CREDIT SECRETS

Master best strategies and techniques to improve credit score and learn most efficient way to get access to business credit

JUNE WISE

Table of Contents

INTRODUCTION 5

CHAPTER ONE: DEFINITION OF CREDIT   7

    1.1 HOW CREDIT WORKS 10

    1.2 TYPES OF CREDIT 10

CHAPTER TWO: WHAT IS BAD CREDIT   12

    2.1 EXAMPLES OF BAD CREDIT 12

    2.2 HOW TO IMPROVE BAD CREDIT 13

CHAPTER THREE: WHAT IS FICO SCORE   14

    3.1 CALCULATING FICO SCORES 15

CHAPTER FOUR: BUSINESS CREDIT VS. PERSONAL CREDIT 18

    4.1 BUSINESS CREDIT SCORE VS. PERSONAL CREDIT SCORE 20

    4.2 CAN YOU USE PERSONAL CREDIT AS A SOLE PROPRIETOR? 21

    4.3 IS BUSINESS CREDIT BASED ON PERSONAL CREDIT? 21

    4.4 DOES PERSONAL CREDIT AFFECT BUSINESS CREDIT? 22

    4.5 DOES BUSINESS CREDIT AFFECT PERSONAL CREDIT? 23

    4.6 HOW TO SEPARATE BUSINESS CREDIT FROM PERSONAL CREDIT 23

CHAPTER FIVE: TYPES OF CREDIT TO HELP GROW YOUR BUSINESS 25

CHAPTER SIX: AVAILABLE CREDIT 29

CHAPTER SEVEN: ACCOUNTS PAYABLE (AP)   32

7.1 ACCOUNTS PAYABLE VS. TRADE PAYABLES 34

7.2 ACCOUNTS PAYABLE VS. ACCOUNTS RECEIVABLE 35

CHAPTER EIGHT: REVOLVING CREDIT AND HOW IT WORKS 35

8.1 BUSINESS AND REVOLVING CREDIT 36

8.2 REVOLVING CREDIT VS. INSTALLMENT LOAN 37

8.3 REVOLVING LINES OF CREDIT VS. CREDIT CARDS 37

CHAPTER NINE: EXPERIENCE AND SHOCKS (A CREDIT SCORE MODEL) 39

CHAPTER TEN: WHAT IS CREDIT SCORING   44

10.1 HOW CREDIT SCORING WORKS 45

10.2 CREDIT SCORING VS. CREDIT RATING 47

10.3 PUBLICLY SUBSIDIZED LOANS 47

10.4 LIMITATIONS OF CREDIT SCORING 50

CHAPTER ELEVEN: HOW TO FIX YOUR BUSINESS CREDIT SCORE 51

CHAPTER TWELVE: HOW TO IMPROVE YOUR CREDIT SCORE 54

12.1 WHAT CREDIT ANALYSTS DO AND HOW THEY WORK 55

12.2 THE FOUR C'S OF CREDIT 56

CHAPTER THIRTEEN: HOW TO GET ACCESS TO BUSINESS CREDIT 59

CHAPTER FOURTEEN: BUSINESS-FINANCING OPTIONS THAT DON'T REQUIRE FLAWLESS CREDIT   63

14.1 WHAT ARE SMALL BUSINESS LOANS FOR BAD CREDIT? 64

14.2 TYPES OF SMALL BUSINESS LOANS FOR BAD CREDIT 64

14.3 PROS AND CONS OF BUSINESS LOANS FOR BAD CREDIT 65

14.4 APPLYING FOR A SMALL BUSINESS LOAN WITH BAD CREDIT 66

CHAPTER FIFTEEN: CREDIT REPAIR 69

CHAPTER SIXTEEN: CREDIT CRISIS AND FAILURE   85

CHAPTER SEVENTEEN: HOW TO GET RID OF CREDIT LOSSES AND ENSURE SAFER BUSINESS 89

17.1 BLAST YOUR BUSINESS CREDIT SCORE! 90

CHAPTER EIGHTEEN: HOW TO CLEAN UP YOUR CREDIT REPORT 93

CONCLUSION 101

REFERENCE............................102

INTRODUCTION

According to Bankrate.com, cash management is one of the most pressing issues facing small companies today, and it can affect everyone. Both failing and thriving firms will run into financial difficulties. Fortunately, building business finance (also known as commercial credit) will assist your small business in obtaining cash when it is needed. Small companies should be careful when it comes to credit: it can help you expand and save you from a bind, but it can also contribute to debt. To avoid ballooning interest rates, you can still use your business credit wisely. Having said that, your small company could greatly benefit from developing business creativity.

More than 65 percent of companies, according to the Small Business Administration (SBA), depend on credit to run their operations. You'll want to purchase products and services on loan as the company grows. Using your personal credit records to fund business ventures is one choice, but it isn't the best. Establish a dedicated line of credit under your business' name, not yours, to optimize your business' ability while mitigating your personal risk. One way an organization determines your creditworthiness is by personal credit. A business will determine how dangerous it is to lend credit to you based on your payment history. The same is true for business credit if your personal credit is in bad shape.

While personal credit is often used to establish business credit, you can establish business credit without relying on your bad credit background. Essentially, just as you establish personal credit based on your personal financial background, you create strategic credit based on how you treat any credit that has been provided to your business, including credit cards, deposits, lines of credit, swap lines from vendors, and more. Company credit, on the other hand, is linked to your workplace identity number, or EIN, rather than your social security number. Finally, just as your personal credit demonstrates your creditworthiness as a borrower, your business credit demonstrates whether or not your company is a reliable borrower.

CHAPTER ONE: DEFINITION OF CREDIT

What do you think about when you hear the word "credit"? In the financial world, credit is characterized as a contract in which a borrower collects a sum of money with something of value and pays back the lender at a later date, usually with interest. Credit refers to a person's or a company's creditworthiness or credit background. It is a bookkeeping entry that reduces assets or raises liabilities and equity on a company's balance sheet, according to an accountant.

A credit agreement is a contract between a lender and a borrower. The creditworthiness or credit history of an individual or a business is also referred to as credit. A credit in accounting can boost assets or increase liabilities, as well as lower costs or improve sales. Schumpeter was pragmatic enough to recognize that in order to operate as an individual, one must collect funds. The capitalist is the one that provides credit. Of necessity, the capitalist will use funds that are the product of active invention and entrepreneurial profit (Schumpeter 1912, p. 72). Since capital use is nothing more than the diversion of inputs of production to new purposes (ibid, p. 116) and since the capitalist absorbs the financial risk (the entrepreneur risks his job and reputation), the capitalist has the power to dictate new production directions (te Velde 2001, p. 7).

Economic development, according to Schumpeter, is a "spontaneous and discontinuous change in the channels of the flow, disturbance of equilibrium, which forever alters and displaces the equilibrium state previously existing" (Schumpeter 1912, p. 64). (ibid, p. 74). Schumpeter emphasized the value of "ad-hoc credit means of payment, which can be backed neither by money in the strict sense nor by already existing goods." Credit serves the purpose of "enabling the merchant to withhold producers' products that he requires from their previous employments by exercising a market for them, and thereby forcing the economic system into new channels" in this way (ibid, p. 106). Credit, according to Schumpeter, provides extra buying power that allows for growth. "Granting credit in this way acts as an order on the economic environment to adapt itself to the purposes of the entrepreneur" (ibid, p. 107). According to de Vecchi (1995, p. 27), the expectation that the entrepreneur will finance his business with investments or previous income is a reasonable one, but it will not produce an adequate return.

Lederer's perspective is in accordance with Schumpeter's claim that someone who desires to act as an entrepreneur in the search of profit must collect funds from the capitalist. Of course, the capitalist will use funds that are the product of creative profit or simply an opportunity for new profit: "Heavy credit market demands are therefore only likely to occur as a result of unexpected opportunities of big profits" (Lederer 1938, p. 230). In this sense, Lederer, like Schumpeter, saw credit as an essential phenomenon of economic expansion: "new possibilities for expanding demand by credit arise" (ibid, p. 230). Indeed, the potential loss of credit in the economy will be disastrous for many businesses (Stern 1938). "Without credit extension, the stagnant sectors will have contracted," Lederer says (ibid, p. 230).

As a result, the absence of credit is the only way to discourage a capitalist enterprise from expanding: "the development of a new mode of production will only be slowed by the lack of additional means of payment" (ibid, p. 224). Often see Lederer (1925, pp. 354-

413). Economic activity is not financed by the savings of the past (i.e. of the recession phase) but only from additional credit (or new savings) which is equal to the creation of supplementary production capacity.

In terms of the market cycle, more credit, according to Lederer, is what counts. "[N]o cyclical development can be explained or defined without taking into account the monetary aspect, additional credit providing the fuel without which any dynamic power can spend itself rather quickly" Lederer's study is strikingly similar to Schumpeter's respective thesis, stressing the discontinuous nature of the need for credit, which is one of the guiding forces of economic growth: "Demands for credit emerge spasmodically on the stock market in the more advanced stages of economic development" (ibid, p. 230).

"Heavy demands on the credit market are thus only likely to arise as a result of sudden prospects of large profits, created in particular by the opening up of new markets, the manufacture of new products, and improved methods of production," Lederer said, emphasizing the importance of innovation in raising credit since technical improvements are the main reason for credit creation on the part of the entrepreneur: "Heavy demands on the credit market are therefore only likely to arise as a result of sudden prospects of large profits, created in particular by the opening up of Technical advancement, on the other hand, may be considered as the primary source of credit requests" (ibid, p. 230). To summarize, both theorists and practitioners place a premium on credit, which they regard as essential to capitalism's working. Credit development was related to entrepreneurship by Schumpeter and Lederer, who saw it as a prerequisite for the adoption of inventions.

1.1 HOW CREDIT WORKS

Credit, in the most basic and widely used meaning, is an offer to buy a good or service with the explicit intention of paying for it later. Buying on credit is what it's called. Credit cards are the most popular means of funding today's transactions. The credit deal now has a middleman: the bank that approved the card pays the merchant in full and extends credit to the customer, who will repay the bank over time. Credit refers to the amount of money a customer or company is available to borrow, as well as their creditworthiness. "He has excellent credit, but he isn't concerned about the bank refusing his mortgage application," for example. Finally, a credit entry in accounting documents a reduction in assets or an increase in liabilities, as well as a reduction in expenditures or an increase in income. In the income statement, a loan raises net income, while a deduction decreases net income. A customer and a service provider, such as a utility, mobile phone, or cable network, enter into a service credit arrangement.

1.2 TYPES OF CREDIT

There are several types of credit available. Bank credit, also known as financial credit, is the most common form. Car loans, mortgages, signature loans, and credit lines are examples of this type of credit. When a bank loans money to a customer, it basically credits it to the creditor, who then has to pay it back at a later date. Credit may also lead to a deduction in the money owed in certain situations. Consider someone who owes a credit card provider $1,000 in sum but returns one $300 purchase to the bank. The refund would be applied to the account as a credit, lowering the balance owed to $700. When a customer uses a Visa card to make a payment, for example, the card is called a form of credit since the consumer is purchasing products with the intention of repaying the bank later.

Financial capital are not the only kind of credit available. In return for a deferred payment, which is a form of credit, goods and services can be exchanged. A type of credit exists where a retailer provides goods or services to a person but does not demand payment until later. When a restaurant receives a truckload of food from a vendor who pays them a month later, the vendor is extending credit to the restaurant. A credit is an entry in personal banking that records a number that has been paid.

Credits (deposits) are traditionally recorded on the right side of a checking account ledger, while debits (money spent) are recorded on the left. When a business orders things on credit, its accounts must report the transaction in multiple ways on the balance sheet from a financial accounting standpoint. Consider the case of a business that purchases goods on loan. The company's inventory account is increased by the value of the transaction (via a debit) after the purchase, resulting in the addition of an asset to the company. However, the balance of the transaction (via a credit) is added to the company's accounts payable area, resulting in a liability.

CHAPTER TWO: WHAT IS BAD CREDIT

Bad credit refers to a person's experience of not paying bills on time, as well as the probability that they will do so in the future. A poor credit score is often the result. Companies may still get poor credit if their payment records and present financial situation are not in good standing. Since they are considered riskier than other borrowers, an individual (or company) with bad credit will find it difficult to borrow money, particularly at competitive interest rates. This is valid of all forms of loans, including both secured and unsecured ones, though the latter has certain alternatives. If a person has a history of not paying their bills, they are known to have bad credit.

A low credit score, typically under 580 on a scale of 300 to 850, indicates bad credit. People with poor credit would have a more difficult time getting a loan or obtaining a credit card. Any people who have either borrowed money or applied for a credit card have a credit file with one of the three main credit bureaus: Equifax, Experian, or TransUnion. The details in those files is used to calculate their credit score, which is a statistic that serves as a reference to their creditworthiness and includes how much money they owe and whether they pay their bills on time. The FICO number, named after the Fair Isaac Company, is the most commonly used credit score in the United States.

2.1 EXAMPLES OF BAD CREDIT

FICO ratings vary from 300 to 850, and borrowers with scores of 579 or lower are generally deemed to have poor credit. According to Experian, nearly 62 percent of borrowers with credit scores of 579 or lower are expected to default on their loans in the future. Fair is characterized as a score between 580 and 669. These borrowers are far less likely to default on loans, making them much less expensive to lend to than those with worse credit ratings. However, borrowers in this range may face higher interest rates or have difficulty obtaining loans than borrowers with credit scores lower to the top 850.

2.2 HOW TO IMPROVE BAD CREDIT

There are steps you should take if you have poor credit (or fair credit) to raise your credit score above 669 and keep it there. Here are few pointers from FICO on how to do just that. Set up automatic online payments for all of your credit cards and loans, or at the very least sign up for the lenders' email or text reminder lists. This would mean that you spend at least the monthly minimum on time. Be wary of "fast fixes" for your credit score that are marketed. There is no such thing, according to FICO. Reduce credit card debt by paying more than the full balance owed wherever possible. Set a reasonable repayment goal and move against it over time. Pay more than the minimum owed will help you increase your credit score if you have a lot of overall credit card debt.

This disclosures are provided by credit card statements. Concentrate on paying down the loans of the highest interest rates first. This will free up the most money, which you will then use to pay off other loans at lower interest rates. Keep your unused credit card accounts open. Often, don't create any new accounts that you don't need. Either action has the potential to damage your credit score. If you haven't used your credit cards in a while, keep them open. Try applying for a guaranteed credit card if you're having trouble getting a regular credit card because of your bad credit. It functions similarly to a bank debit card, with the exception that you can only access the available balance. If you have a bad credit background, using a secured card and making timely payments on it will help you rebuild your credit and maybe qualify for a normal card. It's also a secure place for teenagers to begin building their credit histories.

CHAPTER THREE: WHAT IS FICO SCORE

Try applying for a guaranteed credit card if you're having trouble obtaining a regular credit card because of your bad credit. It functions similarly to a bank debit card, with the exception that you can only access the available balance. If you have a bad credit background, using a secured card and making timely payments on it will help you rebuild your credit and maybe qualify for a normal card. It's also a secure place for teenagers to begin building their credit histories. FICO credit scores are a method of determining and evaluating a person's creditworthiness. Scores range from 300 to 850, with 670 to 739 indicating a "positive" credit history. The FICO scoring methodology is updated on a regular basis, with FICO Score 10 Suite being published on January 23, 2020.

FICO is a software and service provider for both businesses and consumers with a comprehensive analytics framework. The company is most known for creating the most widely used customer credit scores, which are used by financial institutions to decide whether or not to lend money or extend credit. On a scale of one to ten, FICO scores range from 300 to 850. In general, credit scores in the range of 670 to 739 indicate a "good" credit history, which most lenders will appreciate. Borrowers in the 580-669 range, on the other hand, could have a difficult time seeking affordable financing. Lenders weigh a borrower's FICO score when assessing creditworthiness, but they also consider incomes, period of work, and the type of credit sought. FICO scores are useful in a number of cases.

Despite the fact that borrowers can dispute unfavorable things on their credit reports, a poor FICO score is a deal breaker for many lenders. Many lenders, especially in the mortgage industry, have strict FICO minimums for clearance. A rejection occurs if this condition is satisfied by one degree. As a result, there is a compelling case for borrowers to prefer FICO over all other credit bureaus while attempting to construct or boost their credit. You'll need a number of credit cards and a clear payment history to have a high FICO score. Borrowers should also be cautious by keeping their credit card balances within their credit card limits. Given the value of a good FICO score in so many credit decisions, it might also be worthwhile to invest in a good credit tracking service to protect your records.

3.1 CALCULATING FICO SCORES

FICO scores are determined by measuring each category differently for each individual. Payment history accounts for 35% of the score, with accounts due accounting for 30%, credit history period accounting for 15%, new credit accounting for 10%, and credit mix accounting for 10%. In the United States, FICO scores are used in almost 90% of credit evaluations. The key considerations that go into deciding a FICO score are as follows:

a. History of prior payments (35 percent)

Payment history refers to a person's ability to make timely payments on credit cards. Bank documents show the deposits received to each line of credit, as well as any bankruptcy or collection items and any late or missing payments.

b. Accounts receivable (30 percent)

The word "accounts due" refers to a person's outstanding debts. Getting a high level of debt does not necessarily imply a poor credit score. Instead, FICO finds the debt owed in relation to the amount of credit available. A individual who owes $10,000 but has fully extended all of their lines of credit and maxed out all of their credit cards might have a lower credit score than someone who owes $100,000 but has not met the credit limit on all of their accounts. Balance history: when was the last time you used a credit card? 15% of the total. The higher a person's credit score, the more they have had credit. Those with a limited credit history will be able to obtain a positive credit score if they get good grades in the other categories. FICO scores take into account the age of the oldest account, the age of the newest account, and the combined average.

c. Credit distribution (10 percent)

The number of separate accounts you have is referred to as your credit mix. To build a strong credit history, people need a mix of retail accounts, credit cards, installment loans (such as signature loans or vehicle loans), and mortgages. A new line of credit has been created (10 percent). "New credit" refers to accounts that have just been opened. If a creditor opens a significant number of new accounts in a brief period of time, their credit score would suffer. There have been many variations of FICO since the company began revising its estimation methods on a daily basis after introducing the first scoring methodology in 1989. 9 Each upgraded update is sent to each lender, and it is up to them to determine whether or not to execute the change. FICO Score 8, while being supplemented by FICO Score 9 and FICO Score 10 Suite, is still the most commonly used variant in 2021.

In 2016, FICO Score 9 was adopted, with improvements to how medical collection accounts were handled, improved attention to rental records, and a more forgiving attitude to entirely paying third-party collections. Its popularity did not exceed FICO Score 8. However, the addition of trended credit bureau data to FICO Score 10T (part of FICO Score 10 Suite, revealed on Jan. 23, 2020) could lead to it eventually replacing FICO Score 8. FICO score 5 is a lesser-known equivalent to FICO score 8 that is still used for vehicle loans, credit cards, and mortgages. Score 8 is compatible with previous versions, according to FICO, but it has a few unique characteristics that make it a more predictive score than previous versions. FICO Score 8 aims to express how safely and successfully an actual creditor deals with debt, similar to previous FICO score systems. Many who pay their bills on time, hold low credit card balances, and just open new accounts for specific transactions have higher credit scores.

Many that are consistently delinquent, over-leveraged, or frivolous in their credit choices, on the other hand, are given lower ratings. It also ignores collection accounts with a balance of less than $100 at the end. Increased exposure to heavily used credit cards was one of the new features in FICO Score 8, which means that low credit card balances on active cards will have a more favorable impact on a borrower's score. It also handles isolated late fees with more prudence than previous models. If a late payment is an isolated occurrence and all accounts are in good faith, FICO Score 8 is more tolerant, and it splits customers into more groups to have a greater statistical reflection of risk. The main goal of this reform was to prevent borrowers with little or no credit history from being scored on the same scale as those with established credit.

CHAPTER FOUR: BUSINESS CREDIT VS. PERSONAL CREDIT

If you remember what your credit score is? What is the company's credit score? Many more are unaware as well. Furthermore, the majority of individuals do not update their credit score prior to applying for a credit card, a company loan, or a personal loan. Any people are surprised to learn later that they were harmed by mistakes that could have been avoided if they had paid attention. Business credit is determined by the company's financial records and is linked to your EIN number. Personal credit, on the other hand, is dependent on your spending habits and is linked to your social security number. Since these two categories of credit are unique, your company credit score is measured using different factors than your personal credit score, despite the fact that both are basically a numerical evaluation of creditworthiness. Despite their differences, company and personal credit are often linked, and business owners should keep a close eye on both.

All of us are aware that we have personal credit, which is based on our financial spending habits. If you own a small business, though, you can be surprised to hear that you have business credit based on the financial records of your company. Personal and business credit are often confused (especially if you're a sole proprietor), but they're fundamentally separate and should be viewed as such. That said, you may be wondering how these two credit forms connect when it comes to company credit dependent on personal credit. Is personal credit influenced by company credit?

To assist you in making smart financial choices about your small company, we'll clarify the distinctions between business credit and personal credit, as well as address these questions regarding how these two forms of credit compare to one another. We'll also give you advice on how to split your company and personal finances, as well as the credit options that will help you do so.

While business and personal credit are often related, they are distinct, as stated in this book. Despite their common names, these two forms of credit, even though they are for the same individual, represent distinct financial backgrounds. Personal credit, or credit lent to you for personal purposes, such as personal credit cards or student loans, is dependent on your personal spending background. Your social security number is linked to your personal credit (SSN).

The three big credit bureaus, Equifax, Experian, and Transunion, also compile your personal credit background. Each of these institutions has its own profile. Market credit, on the other hand, is dependent on the company's financial background, which includes credit that has been lent to it, such as a business credit card or a small loan. Unlike personal credit, which is linked to your Social Security number (SSN), business credit is linked to your employer identity number (EIN), also known as your tax ID number. You should register for an EIN online if you don't already have one. This amount helps the government to identify your company for tax purposes. It's important to know that you don't technically require an EIN if you're a sole proprietorship with no employees or a single-member LLC with no employees.

Under this scenario, the company's credit will be linked to your Social Security number, and therefore to your personal credit. Company credit, on the other hand, is typically distinct from personal credit. While the three main credit bureaus monitor your personal credit background, Experian and Equifax, as well as other industry-specific monitoring agencies, track your business credit history. Dun & Bradstreet is a well-known business-only credit reporting company. Furthermore, since your EIN is linked to your business credit, your business credit history will accompany you throughout every enterprise in which you use that figure.

Another significant distinction between corporate and personal credit is the extent of which legal guarantees apply. When it comes to your personal credit, you are generally entitled to more civil guarantees. Personal credit rights, for example, allow you the ability to dispute any item on your credit report. In order to comply with fair credit reporting rules, you can ask for incorrect entries on your personal record to be deleted. For company credit, there are no similar rules. You have the right to contest something on your company credit sheet, but the issuer is not expected to respond. As a result, this is just one of the many reasons you should be diligent about your company finances and keep a close eye on your credit report.

4.1 BUSINESS CREDIT SCORE VS. PERSONAL CREDIT SCORE

If you have any questions about how the distinction between corporate and personal credit affects credit scores? Even if both are numbers that reflect creditworthiness, the company credit score and personal credit score are distinct. To put it another way, your personal credit score is a numerical measure of your personal spending history that ranges from 300 to 850, with a higher score suggesting greater creditworthiness. In general, your personal credit score is determined using information from the credit records from the three major credit bureaus, including payment history, debt owing, and duration of credit history, credit forms, and new credit. Your personal credit score is used by banks and insurers to decide whether or not to lend you money. A strong credit score also means you'll be eligible for lower-interest credit. Your corporate credit score, on the other hand, is a numerical assessment of your and your company's creditworthiness, and it's linked to your EIN.

A company credit score usually varies from one to one hundred, with the higher the rating, the more likely lenders, credit card firms, and other forms of lending can extend credit to you. While the system for calculating your personal credit score is fairly consistent, the method for calculating company credit scores varies depending on the credit bureau. However, considerations such as credit usage ratio, payment history, length of credit history, company size, market risk, and so on all impact business credit ratings. It's critical to understand (and improve) your business credit score if you want to expand your company with funding such as a long-term business loan or a low-interest business credit card.

4.2 CAN YOU USE PERSONAL CREDIT AS A SOLE PROPRIETOR?

If your company is a sole proprietorship or a single-member LLC with no staff, your corporation and personal credit will be connected, as we briefly mentioned earlier. If you don't apply for an EIN, your company credit will be linked to your social security number, and therefore to your personal credit. As a sole proprietor, you can use your personal credit, but it's easier to have an EIN and keep these two forms of credit apart. It might seem to be more practical to use personal credit because there is only one way to keep track of charges, and your personal account is likely already created. Unfortunately, as a corporate owner, this exposes you to personal liability if your company runs into financial difficulties. The most significant justification to keep your personal and company accounts apart is to prevent legal responsibility. If the organization has financial troubles, you can be held directly accountable.

4.3 IS BUSINESS CREDIT BASED ON PERSONAL CREDIT?

Is company credit dependent on personal credit the answer to this question? As we've seen, there's a distinction between company and personal credit, but the answer is technically no. However, your personal credit can have an effect on your ability to apply for business credit items in some situations. To clarify, when you apply for a business credit offer, such as a small business loan or a business credit card, your personal credit background is likely to play a big role in your acceptance and the amount of credit you get.

To apply for SBA loans, for example, you usually need a personal credit score of at least 650. You may be wondering why lenders use the personal credit score in their application process if company and personal credit are different. Lenders use your personal credit background as one of the factors in determining the trustworthiness of your company. If you, as the business owner, have decent credit, your business is more likely to repay loaned credit.

4.4 DOES PERSONAL CREDIT AFFECT BUSINESS CREDIT?

This leads to the next question: does personal credit have an effect on company credit? These two terms are, once again, theoretically distinct. However, as previously said, your personal reputation influences your ability to receive business credit items, thus affecting your ability to expand and develop your business credit. Consider the following scenario: you choose to apply for a business credit card in order to establish your company's credit history. The authorizing bank will check your personal credit background as part of the application process. If you have bad personal credit, you will not be eligible for the card, and you won't be able to use this tool to create your company credit (at least not right now). While personal credit is not the only consideration considered when accepting a business credit product application, it may have a significant impact. As a result, before you can work on your business score, you'll need to boost your personal credit in order to apply for this business credit card.

In a similar way, your personal credit background will have an impact on not just the chances of qualifying, but also the parameters of a business credit product if you do. The higher your personal credit history, the more likely you are to get a business term loan with fair terms and low interest rates.

4.5 DOES BUSINESS CREDIT AFFECT PERSONAL CREDIT?

Finally, does corporate credit affect personal credit in the same way as it affects business credit? In some cases, your company credit may have an effect on your personal credit. For example, if you're using a business credit card to establish a credit history for your company and you signed a personal warranty (as certain card issuers require), you'll be kept financially liable for paying even if your company can't, which may have an impact on your personal accounts and credit. Furthermore, depending on the card provider, your business credit card behavior can be disclosed on both your personal and business credit records. These possibilities highlight the importance of keeping a close eye on your business credit and the terms and conditions that apply to specific business credit items.

4.6 HOW TO SEPARATE BUSINESS CREDIT FROM PERSONAL CREDIT

As you can see, while there are subtleties about how business and personal credit are connected, it's important to keep your business and personal finances apart. Separating your corporate and personal accounts (and, by extension, your credit) will help secure your personal assets and liabilities, as well as increase your business loan and credit opportunities.

The easiest way to start separating your company and personal accounts is to open a business checking account, which will help you to hold all of your business funds and pay for business expenses in one place. It would be easier to keep track with your finances and keep company and personal funds apart with this account. Applying for and using a company credit card will also help you keep your personal and business finances apart while still developing a business credit background. A corporate credit card will also help you keep track of your spending which is a perfect way to build positive business credit that will come in handy as your company expands.

While there are distinct distinctions between company and personal credit, the two are inextricably linked. As a result, answers to questions like "does company credit impact personal credit" aren't as straightforward as "yes" or "no." As a company owner, it's important to understand the differences between these two forms of credit and to closely track both your business and personal credit. Setting up a corporate bank account and using a business credit card are both good ways to hold your finances separate, and they will ideally help you build your company's credit history, making future financing more available.

CHAPTER FIVE: TYPES OF CREDIT TO HELP GROW YOUR BUSINESS

If you own a company, there's a fair chance you'll need more small business money than you actually have. Maybe your customers aren't paying on time, or you'd like to expand your business. Or maybe you simply want to stock up ahead of a holiday rush. Whatever the case might be, there are a number different forms of company lines of credit that may assist you. Technically, lines of credit are grants, but with a twist. These finance tools operate similarly to credit cards in that they give company owners a fixed sum of money to use or not use at their discretion. Unlike a conventional loan, the money in your usable capital pool is yours to spend, redeem, and reuse over and over again. When you spend the currency, interest accumulates. You may be able to write checks from your line of credit account, you may need to visit the financial institution, or you may be able to pass money to your business account. While there are only two types of business lines of credit: secured and unsecured, there are also alternatives under both. Starting a new company is a thrilling and fascinating experience. There are too many choices to think and select from. One of the most crucial is the ability to raise the funds you'll need to get off and stay in operation for the long haul. Unfortunately, this can be very distressing, particularly if you are unfamiliar with your choices, such as the various forms of credit. This requires an unsecured vs. insured business line of credit.

a. Secured Credit.

Collateral is used for secured business lines of credit. That is, as a promise, you will put up something of worth, such as company properties or real estate. This assurance tells the lending agency that if you refuse to repay the loan, they will take the assets to fund the debt. Since the cost is smaller, a guaranteed line of credit could have improved overall conditions. The interest rate may be smaller, the maturity terms may be more flexible, and you may be eligible for a larger credit line. When a bank, credit union, or any form of financial institution lends money, they often do so with a protected line of credit. This means that money is loaned to an individual or a company in exchange for some kind of security. Under the case of a revolving loan, the financial institution may be paid until the property is sold if the loan is defaulted on. If the desired credit is in the form of a business credit card, a sum equal to the credit cap is deposited in the financial institution that is extending the credit. The money is kept until the institution decides that the company is no longer a credit concern, at which point it is returned. The money is taken from the institution if the creditor defaults on his credit line.

b. Unsecured Credit.

You won't have to put all of the savings up as collateral on an unsecured line of credit. You can also benefit from a faster approval process. Interest rates are often higher than guaranteed lines of credit, and there may be a monthly or annual servicing charge. Unsecured lines of credit, according to the SBA, can be preferable to protected lines of credit. They place a greater emphasis on creditworthiness than on years of business, and the application process is often simplified. If a company has a strong track record of settling its bills on schedule and in full, the odds of the owners receiving an unsecured line of credit are even higher. If the owner of a new company lacks a credit background, unsecured credit may be given, or unsecured credit may be granted if the owner uses his own personal credit history as a guarantee. A prospective business owner may also be eligible for unsecured loans if he or she submits a business plan along with an application. In such situations, the institution may award an unsecured business credit line based on the merits of the business plan, but this is usually reserved for very limited loans before a positive business credit background is formed.

Once a company has developed a good credit background, it can be given an unsecured business line of credit as well as unsecured business credit cards. Revenues, costs, existing credit, and the number of years the company has been in existence are all considerations that go into determining these unsecured business lines of credit. Consider it like planning a portrait of your business, both before and after obtaining the credit you need. The better the photo, the more likely you are to be given credit.

c. Real Estate Line of Credit.

There's another product to consider whether you're in real estate or want to be. A real estate line of credit is equivalent to a personal HELOC (home equity line of credit), and is a loan dependent on the amount of equity you have in your home. You will use the equity in your house or the equity in other assets you own to secure a loan for commercial purposes. However, there is another way. Secured and unsecured real estate lines of credit are available. The SBA explains that your FICO ranking is the deciding factor on an unsecured real estate line of credit. This encourages you to purchase and flip houses while remaining competitive in the market rather than having to wait for one property to sell before purchasing another.

d. Business Credit Card.

The SBA also suggests using a business credit card as an unsecured alternative. A line of credit is almost equivalent to a credit card, but it comes with a few more benefits. The biggest advantage is that nothing you own, whether for business or privately, is attached to a credit card. You often get immediate access to currency, which is useful because transferring funds from a line of credit may take days. In comparison to lines of credit with fixed monthly payment rates, the payment options are much more flexible. Whatever option you want for your business, there are a few things you can do to increase your odds of having the best price. Maintain strong personal and business credit by not using too many credit cards (and not maxing out the ones you already have), and working to demonstrate profitability.

CHAPTER SIX: AVAILABLE CREDIT

The amount of credit available to a borrower is referred to as available credit. Subtract the borrower's transactions from the account's gross credit cap to arrive at this figure. The account balance of a credit card or other type of debt is proportional to available credit. The amount of available credit applies to how much a borrower has left to spend after subtracting the borrower's expenses (and the interest on those transactions) from the account's overall credit cap.

The credit cap is the cumulative amount that can be borrowed; a consumer's overall credit limit is typically measured by their credit reports and gross annual income. The amount of available credit applies to how much a borrower has left to pay after subtracting the borrower's transactions from the credit account's overall credit cap. When you deduct all of your transactions (and the interest on those charges) from your credit card's full credit balance, unused credit is the sum that remains.

Payments on credit cards and other forms of revolving credit go toward increasing the borrower's credit limit (which the borrower can then use for additional purchases). The discrepancy between the overall credit cap and the amount the creditor has accrued from transactions is known as available credit (in addition to the interest on the amount of their purchases). When you deduct all of your transactions (and the interest on those charges) from your credit card's full credit balance, unused credit is the sum that remains. Accessible credit for credit card holders can fluctuate: It will rise or fall depending on the borrower's purchase and payment history.

At any time, a creditor will review their available credit. The creditor would pay both the principal and the interest on credit cards and most other forms of loans on a monthly basis. Payments on credit cards (and other forms of revolving credit) go toward increasing the borrower's credit limit (which the borrower can then use for additional purchases). When a creditor makes payments on every revolving credit account, even credit cards, and their available credit decreases. When they make deposits, on the other hand, their available credit grows.

As debt is applied to a borrower's account per month, the amount of credit available to them reduces as well. Borrowers get a monthly statement that lists all of their transactions, as well as any debt accumulated over the previous 30 days and the balance due. A borrower's payment rate includes both their principal and interest; a borrower's principal is the amount of debt they have accumulated from transactions. The amount of interest they owe depends depending on the terms of the cardholder's interest.

Available Credit vs. Credit Limit.

Credit cap and available credit are two words that refer to the account balance of a credit card or any kind of debt. The cumulative amount of credit available to the creditor is known as the credit cap.

The discrepancy between the credit cap and the account balance is known as available credit. Available credit determines how much money a borrower has left to spend based on the account's current balance. The available credit number and the credit cap amount will be equal if no transactions have been made. When a creditor consumes all of their available credit, their credit cap is met, and their available credit is void. The borrower's account has been maxed out, and he or she is no longer able to make payments (without exceeding their credit limit). It is in borrowers' best interests to be mindful of their available credit balance at all times.

If they make more transactions and accrue more interest, their debt will rise, bringing them closer to their credit cap. Their expenses will be capped after they've met their full credit limit. A borrower's credit score can be harmed by exceeding a credit account's maximum cap or holding large balances with less available credit (especially when it is done across multiple accounts). When borrowers have accounts that surpass their available caps, credit bureaus usually subtract points from their credit ratings.

CHAPTER SEVEN: ACCOUNTS PAYABLE (AP)

Accounts payable is a general ledger account that represents a company's duty to compensate creditors or customers on a short-term loan. Another general meaning of "AP" is the business department or division in charge of making payments to vendors and other creditors on behalf of the corporation. Amounts owed to retailers or manufacturers for products or services purchased but not yet paid for are referred to as accounts payable. The accounts payable balance on the balance sheet is the sum of all remaining balances owed to suppliers. The cash flow statement shows the rise or reduction in gross AP from the previous year. To maximize cash flow, management can opt to pay unpaid bills as close to their due dates as possible.

The net accounts payable (AP) balance of a company at a given point in time will appear in the current liabilities column of its balance sheet. Accounts payable are loans that must be settled in a certain amount of time in order to prevent default. AP applies to short-term interest obligations owed to vendors at the business level. The payable is effectively a short-term IOU between two businesses or entities. The other side must record the exchange as a corresponding rise in its accounts receivable. In a company's balance sheet, accounts payable (AP) is a critical statistic. If AP grows in contrast to the previous time, it means the organization is purchasing more products or services on credit rather than paying cash. When a company's AP declines, that means it is paying down past time loans more than it is buying new goods on credit. Accounts payable administration is essential to a company's cash flow management.

When preparing a cash flow statement using the indirect form, the top portion, cash flow from operational operations, shows the net rise or decrease in AP from the prior year. To some level, management can use AP to control the company's cash flow. If management needs to boost cash balances for a certain date, they will stretch the time it takes the company to settle all remaining accounts in AP. However, the ability to compensate later must be balanced against the company's existing agreements with its suppliers. Paying bills by the due date is often a sound corporate idea. Both transactions into the general ledger must include an offsetting debit and credit, according to proper double entry bookkeeping. The accountant credits accounts payable as the bill or invoice is received to register accounts payable. The debit offset for this entry is usually to an expense account for the credit-purchased item or service. If the object bought was a capitalizable asset, the debit may also be against an asset account.

The accountant debits accounts payable to minimize the debt balance until the bill is charged. The cash account receives the counter credit, which reduces the cash balance. Consider the following scenario: a company receives a $500 invoice for office supplies. When the payment is sent, the accounts payable department registers a $500 credit in accounts payable and a $500 debit in office supplies cost. At this point, the $500 debit to office supplies expense passes in to the income statement, indicating that the corporation has registered the sales transaction despite the fact that no money has changed hands. This is consistent with accrual accounting, in which costs are recorded as they are accrued rather than when money is exchanged. After the corporation pays the bill, the accountant records a $500 credit to the cash account and a $500 debit to accounts payable.

When a business owes money for services given or goods delivered but has not yet been paid for, a payable is made. This may be due to a cash buy from a retailer, or a subscription or installment charge due after acquiring products or services. Accounts payable appear on a company's balance sheet and are recorded as a current obligation since they reflect money owed to others. Receivables are assets that reflect money owing to the company for services rendered. Accounts payable, on the other hand, reflect money owing to others by the organization. Payments owed to vendors or banks, for example. Liabilities are used to account for payables. Accounts payable is often misunderstood to refer to the regular costs of a company's core activities, although this is an erroneous reading of the term. Expenses appear on the income statement, while payables appear on the balance sheet as a debt.

In every given time, a business can have a range of available payments owed to suppliers. Accounts payable keeps track of the unpaid fees to retailers. As a result, anyone looking at the accounts payable balance will see the gross amount owed to all of the company's suppliers and short-term lenders. The balance sheet indicates the overall number. For example, if the business above had got a $50 invoice for lawn care services, the balance of all entries in accounts payable would equate $550 before the debts were paid off.

7.1 ACCOUNTS PAYABLE VS. TRADE PAYABLES

While several people confuse the terms "accounts payable" and "deal payables," they apply to identical yet distinct circumstances. The money a company owes its sellers for merchandise-related items, such as business products or components that make up the product, is referred to as trade payables. Many of the company's short-term debts and liabilities are accounted for in accounts receivable. If a restaurant owes money to a food or drinks business, for example, the goods are part of the product and therefore part of the exchange payables.

Accounts payable includes duties to other businesses, such as the cleaning firm that cleans the restaurant's employees uniforms. All of these types are used in the larger division of accounts payable, and many businesses lump them together under the name accounts payable.

7.2 ACCOUNTS PAYABLE VS. ACCOUNTS RECEIVABLE

Accounts payable and receivable are the polar opposites of each other. Accounts payable refers to the money accrued to a business's suppliers, while accounts receivable refers to the money owed to the company by consumers. When one entity transacts with another on credit, the first reports an entry in accounts payable, while the second records an entry in accounts receivable.

CHAPTER EIGHT: REVOLVING CREDIT AND HOW IT WORKS

Revolving credit is a type of credit that allows an account holder to borrow money on a regular basis up to a certain amount and repay it in installments. Each payment replenishes the account holder's available funds, minus the interest and fees paid. Revolving credit is the basis of both credit cards and bank lines of credit. In most cases, revolving credit is allowed with no end date. As long as the account is in good faith, the bank will allow the relationship to proceed. The bank can increase the credit limit over time to enable its most loyal customers to buy more. Revolving credit usually has a higher interest rate than regular installment loans because of the ease and affordability. Variable interest rates on revolving credit can be changed at any time. Revolving credit has a wide range of prices.

Customers with excellent credit scores could get a home equity line of credit with an interest rate under 4% as of March 2021. The loan holder's home serves as security for this form of loan, which is effectively a second mortgage. Credit cards, on the other hand, have an annual interest rate of almost 15% for borrowers with excellent credit scores, and it's up to 18% for "starter cards" for young buyers. That doesn't have any costs associated with the account.

8.1 BUSINESS AND REVOLVING CREDIT

Both small and large companies depend on revolving credit to keep their cash flow stable during seasonal variations in expenses and revenue. Rates differ considerably, much as they do for customers, based on the business's lending background and whether the line of credit is backed by collateral. Businesses, like customers, can keep their interest rates down by paying down their balances to zero per month. Customers with revolving loans have the ability to borrow funds up to a predetermined credit cap. When a customer pays off an open balance on a revolving loan, the money is made available to them again, without any interest and fees.

The client pays interest on the existing amount owing on a monthly basis. If the borrower retains the power to reclaim the property if the client defaults, revolving lines of credit may be backed by collateral. Credit Limitation. The credit cap is the overall amount of money that a financial institution can lend to a borrower who needs money. When a financial entity, normally a bank, comes to an arrangement with the client, the credit cap is set. When forming a revolving line of credit, financial institutions can charge a commitment fee. There are also interest rates on open balances for business creditors, as well as carry-forward charges for individual deposits.

Before establishing a credit cap, financial institutions weigh a number of considerations related to the borrower's ability to pay. Credit score, current wages, and job security are all variables that affect a person. The bank examines the balance sheet, income statement, and cash flow statement for an organization or company. A company's revolving line of credit could be secured by its own assets. The overall credit given to the customer in this situation could be limited to a certain amount of the protected asset. A credit cap of 80 percent of inventory balance, for example, may be set by a firm. If the corporation fails to redeem the loan, the financial institution will seize and auction the secured properties to satisfy the debt. Credit cards, home equity lines of credit, and personal lines of credit are also popular revolving credit examples.

8.2 REVOLVING CREDIT VS. INSTALLMENT LOAN

A revolving loan, on the other hand, includes a certain amount of installments, plus interest, for a certain period of time. For revolving credit, all that is required is a minimum payment plus any penalties and interest charges, with the minimum payment determined by the existing balance. Revolving credit is a strong predictor of credit risk and may have a significant effect on a person's credit score. Installment loans, on the other hand, will appear on a person's credit record more positively if all payments are received on time.

A company or person with revolving credit has been pre-approved for a loan. - when you use the revolving credit, you don't have to fill out a new loan application or reevaluate your credit. Revolving credit is designed for smaller, shorter-term loans. Financial institutions require more structure for larger loans, including pre-set installment payments. A provision in a revolving credit arrangement also requires the lender to close or substantially limit a line of credit for a number of reasons, the most serious of which may be a drastic economic decline. It's crucial to know what obligations the lender has under the arrangement in this respect.

8.3 REVOLVING LINES OF CREDIT VS. CREDIT CARDS

The most well-known type of revolving credit is credit cards. A revolving line of credit, on the other hand, differs significantly from a consumer or corporate credit card in a number of ways. To begin with, unlike a credit card, there is no physical card required to use a line of credit; instead, lines of credit are usually obtained by checks provided by the lender. Second, obtaining a line of credit would not necessitate making a transaction. It enables funds to be deposited into a customer's bank account for whatever purpose without the need for the money to be used in a transaction. This is equivalent to a credit card cash advance, but it also does not come with the excessive fees and higher interest rates that a cash advance does.

CHAPTER NINE: EXPERIENCE AND SHOCKS (A CREDIT SCORE MODEL)

Credit scoring is a predictive analysis used by lenders and financial firms to assess the creditworthiness of an individual or a small, owner-operated company. Lenders use credit scoring to help them determine whether to grant or reject credit. Many financial transfers, such as deposits, vehicle loans, credit cards, and private loans, are influenced by a credit score. Credit ratings are used to decide a person's ability to repay money for things like mortgages, car loans, and even private student loans. FICO and VantageScore are two common credit scoring models. Credit scoring is used by lenders in risk-driven pricing, which determines the terms of a loan, including the interest rate, that are provided to borrowers based on the likelihood of repayment.

Individuals and independent, owner-operated businesses receive credit scores, while companies and governments receive credit scoring. For the past few years, credit scoring has been the most important financial development for small businesses. Credit rating is a mathematical method that assesses the chances of a prospective borrower repaying a loan on time based on his or her credit background. Fair, Isaac and Company, which now rents it to big and small financial institutions, created the main scoring model now used. It was developed in the early to mid-1990s. The company's Small Business Scoring Service now has many models that rate different credits in a variety of ways, including loans, lines, minimal data scoring, and credit size scoring.

Wells Fargo, for example, has its own patented versions [Berger and Frame]. Most interestingly, the models' prediction findings tend to be very reliable. [Board of Governors of the Federal Reserve System (2007b)] The Federal Reserve recently filed a study with Congress asserting that credit scoring was indicative of credit insecurity for the general public and all large demographic groups. Though the study does not specifically mention small businesses, often small business owners' personal credit records are essentially the business's credit records [Berger and Frame; Cowan and Cowan; Eisenbeis]. In the 1990s, credit rating was not a novel concept.

It has been used in consumer loans for years. The study that showed that the creditworthiness of a small company was critically related to the creditworthiness of a person for loans less than $100,000 provided the impetus for rating small business loans [Berger and Frame; Eisenbeis]. The opacity of small business has been broken until the link between the person and the business was established.

Credit rating may be a useful method for speeding up credit checks. "Scoring has the potential to be one of the drivers that changes small business banking as we know it," wrote the Philadelphia Fed's Vice President for Analysis at the time [Mester, p. 14]. Credit rating is being used by major banks all around the world, as well as some independent banks in the United States. Because of the accountability problem, small business loans have historically been aligned with small banks and partnership lending. Large banks were able to enter the small business lending industry in a major way thanks to credit scoring. According to a study commissioned by the Atlanta Fed in the late 1990s, 63 percent of major banks use credit scoring on small business loans, with another 11 percent expecting to do so in the coming year [Berger and Frame].

All of the people who got it used it for commercial loans under $100,000, and 73% used it for loans under $250,000. Smaller banks are far less likely to use credit scoring, with the size of the bank being directly proportional to the likelihood of scoring. Cowan and Cowan discovered that 53 percent of their small bank dominated survey [Cowan and Cowan] did not use the methodology. Smaller bank officials cited a variety of factors for their behavior, including loans that are difficult to rate, a lack of trust in credit ratings, low loan volume, cost, and consumer opposition. Credit scoring is used by banks for a variety of purposes. According to the Atlanta Fed poll, 42 percent of credit scorers are "rules" banks, meaning they use credit scores to make accept/reject decisions [Berger and Frame]. Another 32% of banks, known as "discretionary" banks, use credit ratings to determine loan conditions. It is used by a non-exclusive party to keep track of loans that have been extended. After underwriting, the primary application of credit scoring, according to the Cowan and Cowan report, is annual reevaluation of current loans, accompanied by borrower analysis and risk-based pricing. Despite this, only about 20% of scoring banks used it for risk-based pricing, compared to over 30% of those with more than $1 billion in assets [Berger and Frame]. "The extant literature clearly indicates that SBCS has improved small business credit access in a variety of dimensions," Berger and Frame argue [Berger and Frame, p. 17].

According to one report, credit rating raised the portfolio share of small business loans by 8.4%, or $4 billion per bank, among the country's 200 largest banks [Frame, et al. (2001b)]. Another researcher observed that the rises in low and moderate-income census tracts were around seven times higher than in higher-income tracts [Frame, et al. (2001a)]. Berger and Frame also believe that credit scoring has improved lending to less transparent, riskier borrowers, lending to low-income communities, gap in lending, and loan maturity [Berger and Frame].

The growth in in-bank uniformity delighted banks, borrowers, and regulators alike. And small loan processing became more efficient; according to a senior Wells Fargo executive, credit rating helped the bank cut the amount of administrative measures required to approve a small business loan from nearly 50 to just two. More details about borrowers could result in lower default rates and, as a result, lower loan costs. As a result, credit scoring seemed to be beneficial on both fronts. Credit scoring, on the other hand, did not result in a lower price. Rather, it raised the cost of both "rules" and "discretion" banks [Berger, et al. (2002); Cowan and Cowan].

The fact that discretion banks rate and underwrite in the conventional way is one of the reasons. Instead of one expense, two are borne (and passed on). A second cause is expanded credit supply to less-than-$100,000 risky investors [Berger and Frame]. Credit scoring banks, especially rules banks, are essentially cross-subsidizing the risk of small business lending by allowing highly creditworthy companies to borrow small sums to subsidize comparatively weak risks. If loan terms are linked to danger, this does not happen. However, one banker close to the situation told the author that she was worried because too many "amateurs" in the industry refused to change terms for risk. [Berger, et al. (2002)] The learning curve within the market and within organisations is extremely steep. The default rate did not decrease as a result of scoring. Credit scoring, including gap, is linked to higher default rates [DeYoung, et al. (2006)]. Since scoring encourages banks to lend to more vulnerable customers, higher default rates exist. As a result, the practical disadvantage of credit scoring, or the trade-off for better liquidity, is a higher cost for the borrower and a higher likelihood of default for the lender. Without an effective and accurate infrastructure that offers credible and detailed data to measure credit ratings, credit scoring is impossible.

Dun & Bradstreet, Experien, Equifax, and Trans-Union are the four main data providers in the United States. Everything is kept private. The number of companies on which D&B holds company credit records has risen at a rate of over 6% annually over the last three decades, which is 212 times faster than the economy [Rajan and Zingles]. Coordination is just as critical as development. D&B, for example, has partnered with Fair Isaac to improve credit scoring for larger loans (up to $10 million), while Equifax provides data to the Small Business Finance Exchange, a non-profit comprised of 23 of the top 25 small business lenders [Berger and Frame]. The Exchange's goal is to aggregate information in order to minimize theft by people who take out several loans from different sources at the same time. These credit bureaus' databases must not only be extensive, but also precise. They log billions of transactions per year, and errors are unavoidable. According to the NFIB Research Foundation (2007), forty percent of small business owners claim to have checked their business credit record in the last year, and sixty-four percent claim to have checked their personal credit record. Around a quarter of each party considered flaws and expressed their dissatisfaction. The majority of those who protested were pleased with the answer, but their perceptions show that the device cannot function properly without the owners' continued attention.

CHAPTER TEN: WHAT IS CREDIT SCORING

Credit scoring and the models that underpin it are relatively new concepts. As a result, they have not seen a severe recession like the one that occurred in 1981-82. What happens if they do, as they will eventually do? What are the chances that the templates will work? And how well will the models be implemented by the institutions? Nobody does, and that is the crux of the matter. Inside and through organisations, scoring has a steep learning curve [Berger, et al. (2002)]. As a result, in the case of unanticipated scoring issues, bank reactions are likely to be harsh and abrupt.

For "rules" banks, quick answer is more important. Since loan conditions in "rules" banks are less likely to be optimized for relative danger, resulting in cross-subsidized risk, scoring surprises are more likely to result in a class of borrowers being denied access rather than higher-risk individual borrowers. For the time being, at least, there will be a lack of connectivity as well as poor small business risks. For those factors, "discretion" organizations, which are less reliant on scores and have words that are usually risk-adjusted, are more cautious.

Similarly, Basel II requires very big banks to have smaller reserve levels on the portion of their assets invested in small business and retail credits. Three economists at the Swedish Riksbank [Jacobson, et al.] have questioned the calculations that determined small business and retail credit to be better than other forms of credit. Not only are they unsure if these groups pose safer risks, but they still can't change the groups to find ones that are fairly comparable. Furthermore, large banks that stick to Basel II reserve conditions will likely gain a comparative edge in small business loans over large banks that do not; however, community banks will not likely gain the same advantage.

As a result, a segment of major banks is incentivized to lend to small businesses, whereas another category is incentivized to lend to large corporations. The equilibrium isn't immediately apparent. None of this portends doom, but it does mean that banks and regulators should be acutely aware of shifts in scored loans and the implications of Basel II in real time. This is particularly true as the economy shifts abruptly or enters a deep recession. If it hasn't already, a second experience-related factor of credit scoring is expected to appear. Large banks, in particular, usually offer greater financial access to small enterprises through credit scoring by cross-subsidization. A subset of small businesses borrowing less than $100,000, or stronger risks, continues to subsidize a subset of small businesses borrowing less than $100,000, or worse risks. This cross-subsidy would not be sustainable in the long run.

At any point, a bank or banks will completely risk price their scored small business loans, lowering rates for attractive borrowers while boosting prices for less attractive borrowers. As a result, scored loans will be offered to fewer customers as a group, or the bank would have to price risk more actively. Small business loans are less appealing because risk is costly to price. As a result, it's likely that the United States, and perhaps others, are in a stage where scoring provides more credit to small businesses than it can when scoring technology matures.

10.1 HOW CREDIT SCORING WORKS
Your credit report has a huge impact on your financial situation. It

has a big impact on whether or not a lender can give you credit. People with credit ratings of less than 640, for example, are classified as subprime borrowers. In order to pay themselves for taking on more debt, lending firms also charge higher interest rates on subprime mortgages than on traditional mortgages. For borrowers with a poor credit score, they can often need a shortened loan period or a co-signer.

A credit score of 700 or above, on the other hand, is usually considered excellent and can qualify a borrower for a lower interest rate, resulting in them spending less money in interest over the term of the loan. Scores of 800 or higher are considered outstanding. The way credit is scored can vary slightly between credit scoring models. The FICO ranking, developed by Fair Isaac Corporation, is the most commonly used credit scoring method in the financial industry, with more than 90% of top lenders using it. VantageScore, produced by the top three credit-reporting agencies: TransUnion, Experian, and Equifax, is another common credit scoring model. A person's credit score ranges from 300 to 850, with 850 being the best available score.3 Small business credit ratings, such as the FICO SBSS, vary from zero to 300. Five factors have an effect on a person's credit score:

Payment history (35%)

Amounts owed (30%)

Length of credit history (15%)

New credit (10%)

Credit mix (10%)

Furthermore, though each borrower sets its own credit score thresholds, the following are the most common: Excellent: 800 to 850, Very Good: 740 to 799, Good: 670 to 739, Fair: 580 to 669, and Poor: 300 to 579. Company records (including number of employees, revenue, holdings, and subsidiaries) Historical business data, Business registration reports, Regulatory action overview, Business operating data, Market description and data, Public filings (liens, judgments, and UCC files), Payment history and processing information. Credit scoring is used by lenders in risk-driven pricing, which determines the terms of a loan, including the interest rate, that are provided to borrowers based on the likelihood of repayment. In general, the lower the credit score, the better the financial institution's rate. Your interest rate would be lower if your credit score is higher.

Your credit score, which is based on a mathematical study of your creditworthiness, has a significant impact on how much you pay for any lines of credit you take out. A person's credit score will decide the size of an initial deposit required to buy a cell phone, cable television, or power, or to rent an apartment. And lenders look at borrowers' credit ratings all the time, particularly when determining whether to change a credit card's interest rate or credit cap.

10.2 CREDIT SCORING VS. CREDIT RATING
Credit ranking, which is similar to credit scoring, should not be confused with credit scoring. Credit ratings are based on a lettered scale and refer to corporations, sovereigns, sub-sovereigns, and their shares, as well as asset-backed securities. Credit scoring models paint a picture of an individual's credit relationship, and ratings differ (though not dramatically) between the three major credit bureaus. The interest rate for recovery and whether or not the creditor may be eligible for a mortgage or debt question are all determined by a credit ranking.

10.3 PUBLICLY SUBSIDIZED LOANS
The development of credit rating adds an important new dimension to the conventional policy issue of whether the government can provide preferential loans (including guarantees) to small business

borrowers for whom and in what conditions, if any. It also expands on the standard issue by considering whether subsidized loans can be provided to people or businesses with high credit ratings. Except for those developed for social reasons, the underlying presumption of publicly-financed small business loan schemes is that the economy cannot fund creditworthy borrowers; thus, a subsidy is needed to provide small business owners with enough credit. It's a case of business weakness.

Credit scoring lowers, and in some cases excludes, it. The opacity of small, private businesses has historically made small business lending challenging. Since borrowers know too much more about the state of their businesses than lenders (information asymmetry), borrowers have a big advantage over lenders [Stiglitz and Weiss]. Credit scoring, on the other hand, eliminates much of the knowledge asymmetry, enabling lenders to assess a small business borrower's creditworthiness of fair trust. The business failure case quickly erodes as the bank lends and lends with fair trust. The removal or reduction of the main business failure claim necessitates a reevaluation of government supported financing systems. The problem isn't one that can be solved in a vacuum. In the main small business loan schemes in the United States and Canada, there is a divergence of policy outcomes. According to the American Government Accountability Office (GAO), there are "tiny variations" in credit ratings between small business owners who use traditional credit and others who use the SBA's main financing mechanism, the 7(a) loan guarantee program [Government Accountability Office]. The score differential between the two categories was just 1.7 percentage points per ranking band on average. Despite the fact that the SBA disputed the GAO's estimates, the SBA's own calculations indicate that more than two-thirds of 7(a) receivers are at low (not even moderate) risk. Although the situation in Canada seems to be different, the same questions apply. Many in the Canadian Small Business Financing (CSBF) program face a high risk of bank denial, according to Riding et al., though the writers contend that subsidies are important outside the accept/reject judgment [Riding, et al.]. Can and will these creditworthy creditors, who are more numerous in the United States and less in Canada, continue to be subsidized by the government? The impact of competition policy or anti-trust bank restructuring or mergers and acquisitions on small businesses have sparked substantial debate in the United States [Ou]. Despite the fact that the problem is particularly significant to the United States, it seems to be less so in most other developing countries; many have only a few major banks. Individual European countries transferring regulatory authority over their financial institutions to the European Union, however, can necessitate a revision of the evaluation [Degryse]. The Internet, credit scoring, and other technological advancements have altered the concept of "distance" in small business lending. A corollary question arises as a result of the changed distance: what constitutes a market for the purposes of competitive policy or antitrust? This topic has been posed previously [e.g., Petersen and Rajan], but it is still valid. The challenge in analyzing the investor market issue from the viewpoint of a small company is that the gap between the two is widening on occasion, but not often, and more certainly less frequently than not. The banking industry has evolved as a result of technological advancements. However, how much and how much technology has altered bank market areas when they affect small businesses remains unclear. Distance is usually not a concern (except for certain regulators and small banks) as long as a loan application is self-evident; remote and local lenders compete for the small business owner's business. When the loan gets more complex, however, distance becomes important because soft knowledge is almost always required for a decision, let alone for risk-adjusted terms. In order to gain soft facts about a creditor, a local financial institution has a significant advantage [Agarwal and Hauswald]. The competition reverts to a more conventional scale in these cases. Again, distance is important. The condition and needs of small business borrowers determine the appropriate bank market sector, at least for borrowing. Given the wide range of borrowing situations, changes in bank market areas could be more academic than real for all but a limited percentage of the small business population. Nonetheless, the issue is worth exploring, and regulators should keep a close eye on it.

10.4 LIMITATIONS OF CREDIT SCORING

Credit scoring, while it ranks a borrower's credit riskiness, it does not include an estimation of a borrower's default probability; however, it simply assesses riskiness from highest to lowest. As a result of its failure to decide whether Borrower A is twice as dangerous as Borrower B, credit scoring suffers. Credit scoring's failure to clearly take in real economic trends is another intriguing limitation. If Borrower A has an 800 credit score and the country falls through a recession, Borrower A's credit score will not improve until Borrower A's actions or financial condition shifts.

However, in April 2020, FICO launched the FICO Resilience Index in an effort to remedy this shortcoming. It's "built to measure consumers' durability or vulnerability to an economic slowdown and gives insight into which consumers are more likely to default at times of economic stress," according to Experian. It can be delivered with a credit file, alongside the FICO Ratings, which can be used by lenders as another viewpoint in credit decisions and account plans through the credit lifecycle." Credit risk models with more sophisticated features, such as systemic and reduced-form models, are used to estimate default likelihood. Advances in technologies, such as deep learning and other analytics-friendly programming languages, are helping to improve credit risk prediction performance scientifically.

CHAPTER ELEVEN: HOW TO FIX YOUR BUSINESS CREDIT SCORE

A credit score is a number ranging from 300 to 850 that indicates a person's creditworthiness. A borrower's credit score improves the way he or she appears to future lenders. Credit scores are calculated using information such as the number of open accounts, overall balance, and repayment history, as well as other variables. Credit ratings are used by lenders to assess the likelihood of a borrower repaying a loan on time. A credit score is essential in determining whether or not a lender can provide credit.

Most financial institutions use the FICO scoring scheme. Repayment history, loan forms, credit history duration, and an individual's overall debt are all factors of credit scoring. Credit use, or the amount of usable credit that is actually being used, is one measure used in determining a credit score. Closing a credit account that isn't being used isn't necessarily a good idea and it can lower a person's credit score. The Fair Isaac Corporation, also known as FICO, developed the credit score model, which is used by financial institutions. Although there are other credit-scoring programs, the FICO score is by far the most common. A person's credit score can be improved in a variety of areas, including timely loan repayment and keeping debt down.

A business credit score is based on details in a business credit report which tests a company's creditworthiness. Your company's creditworthiness is determined by your business credit score. There are always ways to boost your company credit score whether it is poor or thin. Making on-time and early payments to your banks, lenders, and suppliers is an excellent way to improve your poor or thin company credit score. FICO SBSS, Dun & Bradstreet, Equifax, and Experian are the four big business credit bureaus. Each credit bureau has a somewhat different approach to scoring, but all big business credit scores look at a company's willingness to pay on time.

How Your Score Is Calculated.

FICO SBSS, Dun & Bradstreet, Equifax, and Experian are the four big business credit bureaus. Each credit bureau has a somewhat different approach to scoring, but all big business credit scores look at a company's willingness to pay on time. In the United States, there are three main credit monitoring agencies (Experian, Equifax, and Transunion) that monitor, update, and store customer credit histories. Although the details gathered by the three credit bureaus can vary, there are five major factors included when determining a credit score: Payment history, total debt, credit history duration, credit types, and new credit are also factors to consider. Payment history accounts for 35% of a credit score and indicates whether or not a person pays their debts on time. The total amount owed accounts for 30% of the total amount owed and includes the credit utilization percentage, which is the percentage of credit available to a person that is currently being used. Credit history length accounts for 15% of the score, with longer credit records being deemed less problematic so more evidence is used to assess payment history. The form of credit used accounts for 10% of a credit score and indicates if an individual has a combination of installment and revolving credit, such as car loans or mortgage loans. New credit is worth 10% of a person's credit score, and it takes into account how many new accounts they have, how many new accounts they have applied for lately, which result in credit requests, and when the most recent account was opened. Closing credit cards will lower your score if you have a lot of them and want to close any that you don't need. Gather the cards you don't need instead of closing them. Keep them in separate, labeled envelopes in a safe location. To login and review each of your cards, go online. Check for any balances and double-check that your address, email address, and other contact information are right. Often, make sure none of them are set up for automatic payments. Make sure your email address or phone number is entered in the section where you will get updates. Since you won't be using them, make it a point to search for fraudulent activities on them on a regular basis. Create a note to review them all every six months or a year to ensure that there have been no charges and that nothing suspicious has occurred.

CHAPTER TWELVE: HOW TO IMPROVE YOUR CREDIT SCORE

When information on a borrower's credit report is revised, their credit score increases, and new information may cause their credit score to increase or fall. Here are some suggestions for improving a consumer's credit score: Keep track of the bills and pay them on time: It takes six months of on-time payments to make a significant improvement in your credit score. Increase your credit limit: Call to ask for a credit boost if you have credit card accounts. If your account is in good faith, you should be given a credit limit boost. It's important not to spend this amount in order to keep the credit usage rate down.

If you aren't using a credit card, it's best to avoid using it rather than shutting the account. If you close a credit card account, depending on the age and credit cap, it can damage your credit score. Assume you owe $1,000 and have a $5,000 credit cap spread between two accounts. Your loan usage rate is currently at 20%, which is satisfactory. Closing one of the cards, on the other hand, would increase the credit usage rate to 40%, which would have a negative impact on your credit score.

Work with one of the most reputable credit repair firms: In exchange for a monthly fee, credit repair companies will negotiate with your creditors and the three credit bureaus on your behalf if you don't have time to improve your credit score. Furthermore, with the variety of possibilities that a good credit score opens up, it might be worthwhile to use one of the better credit reporting systems to keep your records secure. Your credit report is a single statistic that has the potential to lose or save you a lot of money over the course of your life. You will get better interest rates if you have a good credit score, which means you can pay less on every line of credit you take out. However, it is up to you, the creditor, to guarantee that your reputation is high enough that you have more borrowing options if you need them.

12.1 WHAT CREDIT ANALYSTS DO AND HOW THEY WORK

A credit analyst is a financial expert who evaluates the creditworthiness of people, businesses, and shares. Scoring organizations have recently been chastised for their role in measuring the dangers of structured goods. We'll concentrate on what they've been doing for a while: scoring sovereign debt. Secondary markets for debt securities are involved, offering up-to-date information on rates, yields, and spreads over riskless debt. Default probabilities are often mapped into credit scores, but bond spreads may also be projected into the same scale.

Credit ratings and spreads tend to be capturing the same thing, but the issue we consider in this paper is what rating agencies can teach us that we can't understand by just looking at debt prices. One probability is that rating agencies and investors have separate sets of results. Consider the example of a small investor who wants to diversify his or her portfolio. It will not be in the best interests of any of these investors to have a big analysis department dedicated to each country's fundamentals. Rather, the investor will depend on a single source of knowledge, such as a rating agency.

Larger investors can have research teams, and brokers that represent a wide number of investors may also have a wealth of information. A second response is that, given the same facts, investors and rating agencies can have differing perspectives. Indeed, as we'll see below, various rating agencies have varying perspectives on sovereigns. They disagree almost as much on ratings as they compromise on rough mappings between the agencies. Another way to express the rating agencies' possible position is to say that ratings and spreads are all noisy signs of real and perhaps unknown deep economic fundamentals. So, given the indications offered by markets, do rating agencies add information? That is the question we answer in this report. This is an important subject not only from the standpoint of empirical research on how economies work, and the market for insight about how to measure money, but also from the standpoint of politics. If rating agencies do not contribute facts, their views are meaningless, and it is impossible to contend that their actions are causing policy concerns. However, if it is discovered that they do add information, their opinions are important, and it is important to know that the credit rating market is functioning properly. The role of rating agencies in the sovereign debt market has been discussed in a number of recent papers. Cantor and Packard (1996) and Afonso, Gomes, and Rother (2007) prove that economic fundamentals can be used to model ratings reasonably well. Several studies suggest that ratings have an impact on spreads, but the big concern is whether ratings have an impact when fundamentals are taken into account. Regressing scores on fundamentals, Eichengreen and Mody (1998) and Dell'Ariccia, Schnabel, and Zettelmeyer (2006) view the mistake as the rating agencies' "opinion." They then demonstrate that this residual is crucial in explaining spreads. Powell and Martnez (2007) repeat these analyses, using a system of equations approach, and arguing that the rating agencies' disagreements are instructive. To put it another way, when one rating firm adjusts a rating and the others do not, the spreads adjust.

12.2 THE FOUR C'S OF CREDIT

Lenders use the four C's of credit (character, capability, money, and collateral) to assess borrowers' creditworthiness. Until lending money, banks scrutinize borrowers, particularly during difficult economic times. The "4 C's of Credit," as they're called to bankers, summarize what they're searching for:

a. Borrower's Character.

The borrower's financial past is referred to as character; in other words, what kind of "financial citizen" is this person or company?

Credit history is often used to measure character, particularly when it is included in the credit score (FICO score). Credit score is influenced by a number of factors, one of which is the number of problems you have. The less problems you have, the better the credit score would be. A high personal credit score (over 700) could be the most critical consideration when applying for a business loan. Payments that are late Accounts in arrears, available credit, total debt, and repayment capacity

b. Capacity of Borrower.

The willingness of a company to raise income in order to repay a debt is referred to as capacity. Since a new company has no "economic track record," it is the most dangerous for a bank to accept. When buying a business, ability is easier to assess, and a company that can demonstrate positive cash flow (i.e., revenue beats expenses) for a long period of time has a fair chance of obtaining a business loan.

c. Capital Assets of Business.

The financial assets of a company are referred to as capital. Machinery and facilities for a production business, as well as food inventory and retail or restaurant fixtures, are examples of capital assets. Banks accept money, but with caution, that if the company collapses, they will be left with properties that have depreciated in value, and they would sell at liquidation value. You can see that cash is the best tool for a bank.

d. Collateral to Secure the Loan.

A company owner's collateral is the cash and properties he or she pledges to secure a loan. In addition to having strong ratings, a demonstrated capacity to make profits, and business assets, banks will frequently ask a business owner to guarantee personal assets as collateral for the loan. Banks demand collateral and they don't want the business owner to lose out if the company loses. If a company owner didn't have to put up any personal properties, he or she could just walk away from a failed business and let the bank take what it can from the assets. As banks reason, putting collateral at risk motivates a business owner to work harder to keep the company afloat. If you can see, the old adage "banks just lend money to those who don't need it" holds true in most cases.

You must have an excellent credit record in order to obtain a business loan. Be willing to demonstrate that the company can produce enough money to repay the bank loan, that the business assets have value in case they need to be sold to repay the bank, and that you will pledge your personal assets if the business fails. In certain situations, it might be simpler to simply take your own money and start your own company.

CHAPTER THIRTEEN: HOW TO GET ACCESS TO BUSINESS CREDIT

If you can see, the old adage that "banks just lend money to those who don't need it" holds true in most cases.

You would need an excellent credit record in order to get a business loan. Show that the company assets have worth in case they need to be sold to pay off the bank, and pledge your own assets if the business collapses. It could be cheaper in some situations to simply take your own money and start your own company.

You'll need a good credit history to apply for loans from financial institutions as well as lines of credit from vendors and suppliers, whether you're starting a new business or looking to expand an existing one. Establish credit in your company's name rather than your own to keep your personal finances separate from your business dealings. By demanding a D-U-N-S number from Dun and Bradstreet, you will easily create your company as its own financial body. It would take three to six months to construct your credit sheet, much like personal credit. Credit conditions for small businesses in the United States have been steadily declining for the past two years.

Over the time, credit markets became increasingly difficult for small business borrowers to enter as overall economic conditions deteriorated, the latter worsening in the last 12 months. It was the same story from July to September. In fact, rather than spiking in September to mean that an incident like the bankruptcy of Lehman Brothers or the loss of Fannie Mae and Freddie Mac jolted a steady trend off track, the stolid downward pattern credit conditions have shown over the past months is consistent with the usual end of a market cycle. This is supported by data from both the borrowers' and lenders' perspectives.

From the perspective of borrowers, credit availability data shows an uncanny parallel between the course and level of credit conditions entering the 1990-91 recession and the current period. These figures show that credit is becoming increasingly difficult to obtain over time. September turned out to be more of the same. Less credit demand went hand in hand. Credit conditions are tightening and loan demand is declining, according to lender data (Exhibit 6). Unfortunately, the lender sequence does not cover the period leading up to the 1990-91 crisis, so no comparisons can be made between it and the present scenario. However, the lender's view spans the period leading up to the 2001 crisis, and the parallels between that period and the present situation are striking. For present purposes, the disparity in survey findings is that the lender side emphasizes credit market tightness, while the borrower side emphasizes lower demand.

However, these events are usually associated with the conclusion of a business cycle. Sales slow, balance sheets deteriorate, and the owner's ability to raise inventories and/or make capital improvements wanes as a business cycle comes to an end. That also means the demand for credit is decreasing as lending conditions tighten (or should), and small businesses' ability to handle additional credit decreases. That has occurred, especially in the last year. When liquidity becomes more scarce than it once was, so has the standard uproar of "credit squeeze." Although it's impossible not to sympathize with those who have been taken off guard by shifting circumstances, such issues are signs of a larger problem: low sales and a declining economy. Small business owners are much more worried about "Poor Sales," another indicator of the business cycle ending, and inflation than they are about credit, according to survey results (Exhibit 1). Poor Sales was cited by 20% of respondents as their single most pressing issue in September, while Finance & Interest Rates was cited by 4%.

The question is not whether credit tightens at the end of a business cycle, but whether it can. Lenders are requiring more leverage, and cash flow-based financing is becoming more difficult; personal guarantees are becoming more common; and credit lines are being cut, even as liquidity is still flowing. In September, 33% of small business owners said they could get all of the credit they needed, compared to 6% who couldn't; the rest said they didn't want credit [NFIB Research Foundation, series a]. This is perfectly natural and not at all bothersome. As the cycle shifts into a more optimistic mode, the question is whether the small business credit markets will recover to their previous state.

Despite media reports to the contrary, there is no suggestion that creditworthy small companies are systematically unable to access credit due to frozen credit markets. Certainly, the survey evidence presented above refutes the notion of a serious credit crunch. If small businesses faced those difficulties, the Small Business Administration's 7(a) loan insurance scheme would likely be oversubscribed. After all, the program's goal is to provide loans to creditworthy companies who are unable to obtain credit in traditional markets, with the guarantee offering clear incentives for participating lenders to move credit away from other prospective customers and into small businesses. As a result, 7(a) seems to be the only option for dealing with the new credit freeze – if one exists. Nonetheless, between October 1, 2007 and October 1, 2008, the SBA loan guarantee scheme saw a 30% drop in applicants, with a

50% drop in September 2008 compared to September 2007 [Hess].

The SBA's associate administrator for capital access, Eric Zarnikow, says the agency is seeing less pressure and that its phone and e-mail traffic (from people requesting financial assistance) is under regulation. Small business supporters are concerned that the situation will improve. However, weak sales and a deteriorating economy prevent borrowing for the time being, particularly though some American small business owners feel the credit pains that come at the end of a slump rather than a credit market lock.

CHAPTER FOURTEEN: BUSINESS-FINANCING OPTIONS THAT DON'T REQUIRE FLAWLESS CREDIT

Mel Feller acknowledges and knows firsthand that there are a variety of explanations that a conventional business loan from a bank or credit union might be refused. Your company credit profile is one of the most common grounds for loan denial. Also companies with high growth and profit margins may be turned down for a loan if the lender is concerned about the company's credit score. When a company owner's credit is turned down for a loan, he or she has a few options.

Although some entrepreneurs are able to use personal assets such as home equity and retirement accounts to hold their companies afloat, this is not necessarily the right option. Consider any of these business-financing solutions that don't need perfect credit until you risk wasting those valuable assets.

14.1 WHAT ARE SMALL BUSINESS LOANS FOR BAD CREDIT?

Business loans have a wide range of terms, conditions, and maturity lengths. As a result, many of these financing options don't put as much emphasis on credit scores as some. We've assembled a list of some of the best financing solutions for companies with poor credit to help you choose the one that's perfect for you.

14.2 TYPES OF SMALL BUSINESS LOANS FOR BAD CREDIT

a. Merchant Cash Advance.

You could be a suitable choice for a merchant cash advance if your company has a high number of credit/debit card transactions. You sell a share of your potential credit/debit card sales to a third party in return for cash you will spend straight away with a merchant cash advance. The third party then takes a share of your daily credit card purchases before the advance is fully repaid, plus interest. Since retailer cash advances are seen as a transaction rather than a loan, they can be a viable alternative even for companies with poor credit.

b. Invoice Factoring.

You may be a successful choice for a merchant cash advance if your company has a high number of credit/debit card transactions. A merchant cash advance helps you to sell a percentage of your upcoming credit/debit card sales to a third party in return for cash. The third party then takes a share of your daily credit card purchases before the advance is repaid in full, plus interest. Since retailer cash advances are seen as a transaction rather than a loan, they can be a viable alternative for even the most credit-challenged companies.

c. Invoice Financing.

While invoice funding and invoice factoring are identical, they are not the same. Though invoice factoring entails selling your unpaid invoices to a factor, charge funding merely entails obtaining a loan dependent on the value of your unpaid invoices. Your clients want to pay you on a regular basis.

d. Equipment Financing.

To function, all companies need equipment. Equipment loans enable companies to obtain the equipment they need without incurring a high upfront expense. Since these loans are backed by the equipment, lenders can be more generous in their conditions, including the credit score of the borrower.

e. Microloans.

A business can only require a small sum of money at times. Microloans are an alternative for entrepreneurs, young companies, and businesses that have never borrowed from a bank before. While certain forms of business loans are meant for existing businesses with high credit ratings, microloans are an option for startups, young businesses, and businesses that have never borrowed from a bank before. Microloans are a form of short-term loan since they are for such small sums of capital.

f. Equity Financing.

Few company owners choose to seek equity capital rather than dealing with banks or credit unions to obtain the funds they need. When you find investors for your venture, they become part owners of the company. Rather than your credit score, investors would be more interested in your growth strategy and long-term priorities.

14.3 PROS AND CONS OF BUSINESS LOANS FOR BAD CREDIT

Short-term loans are one of the most common forms of loans available to companies with poor credit ratings. These loans have higher interest rates and are for lower sums of money because they have shorter terms than conventional company loans. While the funds you gain from a short-term loan can be used for a variety of things, since they are short-term loans, they are better suited for dealing with transient cash-flow interruptions and short-term growth programs, rather than large investments. And if the conditions of the forms of business loans for poor credit aren't ideal, paying them off on time will help you increase your credit score, allowing you to get a bigger loan for better terms later.

14.4 APPLYING FOR A SMALL BUSINESS LOAN WITH BAD CREDIT

The application process for a merchant cash advance, invoice factoring, or invoice lending is faster and smoother than applying for a typical business loan. Borrowers with short-term loans will normally keep track of their finances and file corporate tax returns, among other things. A copy of your driver's license or other government-issued documents, as well as your company's license or certificate P&L statements.

Before I go any further, Mel and I need to talk about financials and how important they are in the loan process. When it comes to money, it seems that there are two types of business owners: those who grasp every metric, where it came from, what it means, and what they can do about it, and those who are befuddled by accountant jargon and a sea of numbers and tend to ignore it all. While that may is more comfortable to be the kind of business owner that is disconnected from their finances, it may be detrimental to your performance and hinder you from receiving the money you deserve. In my company, I used to be the second form of owner.

My financial strategy was to increase my earnings until I was so rich that I didn't have to worry about anything else. While and profits and being wealthier are still vital aspects of my strategy, our financial reporting has given me more power, and as a result, I've started to see much better results. In fact, my company went from dragging on vendor invoices for 60 days to reaping good profit in just two years. How did we manage to do it? By strengthening our accounting and having a clearer view of our P&L (Profit and Loss) statement, we were able to achieve our goals. I understand your point of view. Isn't it true that it discloses profits and losses? Yes, however a clear understanding of your P&L assertion will show that you will alter your strategy to increase P and decrease L. Here are the key things on a P&L that can teach you what you need to hear about your company's health.

a. Revenue.

Have you ever asked why the "top line" is often referred to as income? That's because it's the first line on a profit and loss statement, and it includes all of the revenue you've made for your product or service over the year. This does not necessitate the use of grants or cash infusions; only the proceeds from the services provided are included. What does this have to do with anything? As soon as you start monitoring your performance on a regular basis, you'll be able to see if you're up or down. Up means fine, so keep improving what you're doing; down means bad, so figure out what you're not doing well and, if possible, improve your marketing budget.

b. Cost of Revenues.

This is the controllable cost of delivering a business to the consumer, and it's included in the spending column of the P&L. Usually, this applies to the prices of goods as well as the labour involved with them. In our business, we like to think of it as a percentage and aim for 55%. If we have a month where our cost of supplies has increased dramatically, we know we need to check at our distributor invoices and see what costs have increased and immediately negotiate them back down, sometimes receiving retroactive credits for the unannounced increases.

c. Income from Revenues.

This is my favorite line because it shows you whether or not your core company is profitable. If the number is positive, you are doing well and will continue to rise. If the answer is negative, it's time to enter triage mode and figure out what's wrong. And if this figure is positive, your company might also be losing money due to all the other costs that are yet to be paid for, such as electricity, mortgage fees, and taxation, but this number will inform you if your basic idea is sound.

Your P&L statement will give you a nice snapshot of the health of your company and help you make more calculated choices, whether you're a seasoned vet in the business world or just getting started. If you've spent some time with them, you'll begin to anticipate seeing them and seeing the patterns in the figures. Take control of your profits and expenses because they are critical to your company's growth. Now, in terms of equity funding and microloans, more time and commitment would be needed to plan. Anyone considering investing in your business would like to see a comprehensive business strategy.

Furthermore, just because microloan lenders are more likely to lend to small enterprises and businesses that are unable to obtain loans from a bank does not mean that microloans are easy to obtain. If you're applying for a microloan, the lender may like to know about your business plans, how you plan to use the loan, and how it will really help you become more successful.

CHAPTER FIFTEEN: CREDIT REPAIR

Bank repair offers a number of advantages, including the ability to provide more loans at cheaper interest rates and with more attractive repayment conditions. When you repair your credit, you'll be in a better shape to accomplish your objectives. Better credit scores widen your opportunities, whether your aspirations are personal, such as purchasing a new home, or enterprise, such as expanding your company. That is why, before you need to borrow money or bid on a new project, now is the time to repair your bad credit. This credit restoration advice will help you boost your credit in a short amount of time. With poor credit, navigating today's world is challenging. A lot of businesses use your credit to determine whether or not to do business with you, as well as to determine the price of goods and services you use. Credit restoration is often sought by consumers with a poor credit background in order to boost their financial status. Here are the most important things to consider when you weigh your choices.

1. You Can Do It Yourself.

Although a respectable credit restoration firm might be an alternative for certain individuals, there's nothing they can do for you that you can't do for yourself. There's lots of material available in books and on the internet that you can use to educate yourself on how credit works and what you can do to fix your own credit. Removing derogatory information, for example, can be accomplished with tactics like credit report disputes, debt validation, pay for deletion, and goodwill letters the tools credit restoration firms use to get negative information deleted from your credit report. Not only can doing it yourself save you money, but it will also give you more leverage and influence over your credit history. If you've learned how to fix credit, you'll be able to use them if it's required in the future.

2. Check Your Credit Reports.

To repair bad credit, you need to know your credit score, and the easiest way to do that is to review the credit reports with Experian, Equifax, or Transunion. For personal credit, many businesses have free credit reports, but company credit ratings are a different story. First, each of the three credit bureaus, Dun & Bradstreet (D&B), Experian, and Equifax, has its own scoring model and report forms. Second, most credit reports for businesses are not free. Experian, for example, charges $39.95 for a single standard credit check, while Equifax charges $99.95. Nav.com, a credit reporting website, provides free credit report copies from Experian, Equifax, and D&B.

3. It's not for your credit score, but for your credit report.

The details on your credit report has an effect on your credit score. This is why the first step in fixing your credit is to update your credit report. Visit AnnualCreditReport.com to receive a complimentary copy of your credit check from one of the three main credit bureaus: Equifax, Experian, and Trans Union.

4. Your Credit Score Shows Where Your Credit Stands.

Pay attention to your credit score; it can tell you whether your credit is good, bad, or improving. A low credit score denotes a credit history that needs to be improved. It's a sign that your credit history is changing as your credit score rises. Buying your credit score any time you want to see where you stand will quickly add up. You can track your credit progress for free by using a free credit score service like Credit Karma or Credit Sesame. Look for a credit management program that does not require a credit card when you sign up. Otherwise, you could be signed up for a free trial subscription that would start billing you every month if you don't cancel the plan. Payment history, debt number, credit history age, credit account forms, and recent credit applications are all factors that go into determining the credit score. Your credit score would rise as you improve your credit in any of these regions.

5. It's difficult to get rid of accurate negative information.

It's worth remembering that the term "accurate" is capitalized. Only lawfully obligated credit bureaus are required to erase misleading or unverifiable records from your credit report. It's more difficult to delete correctly recorded derogatory details from the credit report and the credit bureaus are within their rights to do so. In reality, credit bureaus must record all correct facts, including derogatory information, in order for the credit system to function properly. A settling account for a loan you owe is one of the mechanisms for removing accurate negative information. These methods can take longer and require more initiative than a simple credit report disagreement. The better choices for these forms of accounts are debt validation (for settlement agencies), pay for delete, and goodwill deletion requests.

6. It's possible that doing nothing is a strategy.

Bad evidence does not last indefinitely on the credit sheet. The majority of derogatory records on your credit report will be removed after seven years. There are a few exceptions to this rule. Unpaid tax liens and Chapter 7 bankruptcy will sit on the credit record for up to ten years. If an account is approaching the credit reporting time limit, waiting for it to slip off could be less frustrating and time-consuming than attempting to delete it using dispute letters or other methods. Taking action on a derogatory record would not increase the credit reporting time period, contrary to common opinion. For example, if you pay off a six-year-old debt set, it will not be removed from your credit history after seven years. Paying sets are not used with some newer iterations of the FICO and VantageScore credit scores.

7. Closing Accounts Won't Make a Difference.

It's a common misconception that only open accounts are used on a person's credit report, and that closing an account would erase it. Unfortunately, closing an account may have a negative impact on your credit score in some situations. It is not possible to delete an account from your credit report by closing it. All information about the closed account, as stated by your creditors, will remain on your credit sheet. In an email interview with The Balance, Nancy Bistritz-Balkan, former Director Public Relations and Communications of Global Customer Solutions at Equifax, says, "Before closing accounts, customers can take into consideration other considerations that compose credit ratings, such as the amount of time the account has been available." One of the three big credit bureaus is Equifax. "If you've shown the right kinds of actions for an account for a set amount of time (i.e., paying on time every time), closing the account may not make sense." Leaving the account open will actually help you fix your credit if the account is in good standing or can be taken back into good standing by paying off the past due balance. To increase your credit score, you must have free, active accounts and a good payment history. With a poor credit score, opening new accounts can be tough, but rehabilitating the accounts you already have open can be a way simpler.

7. Credit Repair Firms Are Often Untrustworthy.

Many credit repair businesses make lofty commitments they can't keep, charge advance rates, and then refuse to deliver. Both of these are illegal under federal legislation, but customers who are oblivious of the law do not know they are being abused until it is too late. The Federal Trade Commission has been pursuing scores of credit restoration firms who have violated the rules over the last few years. These businesses are often fined and, in some cases, barred from doing business in the credit restoration sector. The below are few red flags if you're dealing with a shady credit repair company: they demand payment in advance before any services are provided, claim a government affiliation or exclusive relationship with the credit bureaus, promise a specific credit score, promise to delete accurate information from your credit report, fail to inform you of your right to dispute information directly with the credit bureaus, or ask you to provide personal information.

8. You can't expect to see results right away.

Rebuilding a poor credit history takes time. Your more recent credit history weights in more heavily on your credit score than older items. A good credit history will usually have few negative entries and a lot of recent positive credit information. A couple months of on-time payments is a good start, but it won't immediately get you excellent credit. Your credit will steadily increase as the negative information falls off or becomes older, and you replace it with better information. As the details in your credit report changes during the credit repair phase, your credit score can fluctuate. Instead of focusing on frequent variations, consider the overall pattern of your credit score over time.

9. Change Your Habits to Protect Your Improved Credit.

Many people go through credit restoration, whether they do it themselves or hire a business, in order to be able to repay money, such as for a mortgage or a car loan. This isn't a problem at all.

However, if you want your good credit to last, you must develop credit-building habits. This means borrowing just as much as you can afford to repay (and maybe even a little less). One of the easiest things you can do with your reputation is to pay your bills on time. "When it comes to creditworthiness, a perfect rule of thumb to note is to settle the bills on time every time," Bistritz-Balkan says. Lenders and borrowers deserve to see that you've always met your contractual obligations on schedule. As a result, paying bills on time is a crucial, basic habit to develop early on." It's necessary to be careful as the process of repairing bad credit takes time. The time it takes varies from person to person, based on the details on your credit report and how you go about repairing your credit.

10. Register your business.

The owner of a small company also finances the loan himself. When you are the company owner, your financial background, which covers your mortgage and auto loans, would have a strong effect on the interest rate on a business loan. You must have an existing, registered company before applying for a business line of credit. You must choose a legal name for your company and categorize it as a sole proprietorship, association, or entity. You must incorporate your small company as a legal entity, register your business name, and acquire a federal tax identification number, also known as an Employer Identification Number, in order to register it (EIN). The EIN of a corporation behaves similarly to a person's social security number, serving as a personal identity for government purposes. Check out the SBA's 5 Steps to Registering Your Business for more details. It's worth noting that each state has its own set of rules for registering a small company.

11. Start a business bank account.

Banks tend to offer a business line of credit to a firm that has a strong credit background. To apply for business credit, you would usually require a two-year-old business bank account. As a result, you can open a company bank account right away. Company bank accounts assist with the development of business credit (as opposed to personal credit history), as well as the separation of personal and business expenses.

12 Build business credit history.

You have a financial history that leads to a credit score, which is basically a record of your debt repayment history. Businesses, like humans, have a credit background and a credit score, and business credit bureaus have these vital reports. Check with the business credit bureaus to see if your organization is classified once you have an EIN. Dun & Bradstreet, Experian Company, and Equifax Business are three major business credit bureaus. The bank will meet with these bureaus after you apply for a business line of credit to assess your credit worthiness. Almost all of your business expenses, such as using your business credit card or creating credit with suppliers, will help you create business credit. If you don't keep your balances down and pay them off on time, you'll have a hard time getting a company line of credit in the future.

13. Apply for a business line of credit.

You will be ready to apply for a business line of credit after you have established a solid credit background. Before you apply, compare the interest rates and conditions offered by various potential lenders. A summary of your annual gross earnings, your company history, and bank records are all required as part of the application process. Lenders will evaluate your credit worthiness while evaluating your submission. According to the Federal Reserve Bank of New York, banks would consider the "Five C's": capacity to repay, cash, equity, requirements (loan purpose), and borrower character. The personal accounts of small business owners would also be included. As a result, bear in mind that your personal credit background is used to create a business line of credit. A corporate credit card lends prestige to the organization and aids in the establishment of decent business credit or the improvement of business credit scores. It's also a way to keep company and personal spending apart. Putting all of your corporate transactions on a dedicated card comes in handy during tax season, making calculating deductions even simpler. Make minor payments using the new credit card, just like you would with a personal credit card, then pay the account off in full per month. Go on like this for a few months to build a track record of making prompt payments on new credit. When you need money to expand your company, this phase establishes your creditworthiness. Simply ensure that the current credit card issuer reports to a corporate credit bureau. Here's another excuse to get a new company credit card. And if the hard investigation will have a short-term impact on your personal credit score, the company line of credit is different from your personal credit. That is to say, whatever happens to your business card should have no effect on your personal credit score.

14. Add Positive Trade References.

Doing business with "trades" that report to business rating agencies is another credit-repair tactic. Payment data is not shared by all manufacturers and retailers, but the bureaus will tell you which ones do. Dun & Bradstreet needs a minimum of three trade comparisons to determine the PAYDEX ratings, which you can provide. A poor credit score can lead to higher interest rates, lower debt amounts, or the failure to collect funds. That is why you should have "positive" references, or others who can assist you in establishing good credit.

15. Stay patient.

It can take a long time to create credit for your brand. You may have to deal with a lot of red tape. If the process can be aggravating, try to be vigilant and invest wisely. A business line of credit might be the help your small business wants one day. Several things influence your company credit score, including debt repayment history, liens, bankruptcies, and more. You have a pattern of payment defaults if you have a low business credit score. Thin credit, on the other hand, refers to a lack of company credit records that can be used to assess creditworthiness. Poor and thin credit will have an impact on your business dealings, especially when applying for a loan. You might, for example, only be available for poor credit business loans rather than better-term loans.

It's crucial to find opportunities to boost or construct your business credit in order to improve the facts on your credit report and, as a result, your credit score. It's impossible to build or improve your credit overnight. There are, however, quick steps you can take to help recover your credit.

16. Don't Mix Your Business and Personal Finances.

Your corporation should be viewed as a distinct entity from your personal affairs. Your personal credit, for example, should have no bearing on your company credit. You may do this by establishing two different accounts, one for personal use and the other for business purposes. This has the additional advantage of assisting you in keeping track of and managing both your personal and company finances.

17. Pay Your Bills on Time.

A pattern of late payments has the most negative impact on a credit report. One of the most significant factors affecting your company credit score is your payment background. If you wish to maintain a high credit record, you must pay all of your vendors and lenders on time. The longer a bill is overdue, the lower your company credit score would be. Similarly, if you pay your bills on time, you can be able to boost your company credit score even further. Payment history makes up 35% of the FICO Score, which is used in 90% of credit decisions, according to Experian. Late payments will affect your credit score for up to seven years. Furthermore, their appearance on a credit report, including the total amount, the length of time they were late, and the date they occurred, is linked to potential credit risk. People who have never missed a bill are much more likely to do so in the future. A bill can now be considered past due after 15 days on your credit card or loan statement.

A bill isn't considered past due for credit reporting purposes until it's been 30 days. Once you've missed the deadline, your creditors have the option of reporting you to the credit bureaus, which would have an effect on your creditworthiness. Make paying your creditors on time a priority every month. Even if you have a history of late payments, you will begin to establish reputation, which will eventually lead to higher credit scores. Keep track of your payments and compensate those who are nearest to the 30 day mark first. Setting reminders is a great way to make sure you don't forget to make a payment. This can be done in a number of ways. Your computer or mobile device's calendars, Reminders from your bank or credit card company via text or email Payments are made automatically from your company bank account. If you choose the last choice, make sure you have enough money to cover the draft. Overdraft fees can eat into your balance and can harm rather than improve your credit score.) pay off as much business debt as possible. Consider this straightforward credit-repair technique. Just pay off the lowest balance or pay off the account with the highest annual percentage rate. Assume you have two accounts to pay. This can be accomplished in a number of ways. Calendars on your screen or mobile device are a great way to stay organized. Reminders from your bank or credit card issuer via text or email Payments are made automatically from your business bank account. Make sure you have enough money to cover the draft if you want the last choice. Overdraft fees will eat away at your balance and can harm rather than improve your credit score.) pay off as much business debt as possible. Consider this basic credit-repair technique. Pay down the account with the largest annual percentage rate first, or pay off the account with the smallest balance. Assume you have two accounts to pay on.

18. Build Credit with Vendors.

It's important to cultivate positive working relationships with the vendors and suppliers so that they can report on-time and early payments to the credit bureaus. However, this isn't something that all vendors do automatically. It's a smart idea to select suppliers and borrowers who can report on timely payments to credit bureaus.

19. Keep Your Credit Utilization Ratio Low.

Most companies that are unable to obtain business loans use business credit cards to establish credit. Using a business credit card while maintaining a low credit utilization ratio can improve the credit report and score. A monthly credit utilization ratio of less than 33% is optimal. Credit usage rates on both personal and company credit cards must be kept low by small business owners. It's best to keep the percentage below 30%. This is significant because, after payment history, credit utilization is the second most important factor in credit scores.

The number of all your credit card balances is divided by the amount of all your credit card limits to determine your credit utilization rate. It's in your best interest to keep your credit utilization below 7%. This places you in the 740-799 credit score range, which is considered "very strong." Even better, keeping it between 1% and 3% will get you an 800-850 "exceptional credit" ranking. However, do not have a credit utilization rate of 0%. If all of your credit cards have no balance, you aren't building credit. In fact, it's likely that your score would be lower. So, while you can use both your company and personal credit cards and lines on a regular basis, you should also pay them off or off early each month.

20. Check Your Credit Reports and Ensure Accuracy.

Check your credit reports on a regular basis to ensure that the information listed is correct. Any incorrect data must be corrected by the company. When it comes to disputing errors, each credit reporting agency has its own set of rules. Correcting errors in the report takes a month or more, so you might as well do it now while you still don't need it. Check your personal credit score on a regular basis for any changes. Your objective should be to reach a score of 633 or higher. You might be surprised at how much of a difference even small improvements can make.

Scores are updated on a monthly basis by the reporting agencies, so check at least once a month. Additionally, some credit reporting agencies will send you an email whenever your credit score changes. If those are available, sign up for them. Personal credit monitoring services usually offer advice on how to raise your credit score, and some even keep track of your spending. Establishing a baseline and then tracking changes, just like any other metric, will put you on the road to credit repair success. Business credit reporting agencies, in addition to individual credit reports, offer annual subscription plans that allow you to check your credit history, credit report, and score for one low price. The fees can be in the hundreds of dollars, but it's a good way to keep track of your credit score and evaluate your credit repair efforts. When you need to finance commercial real estate, office equipment, or another business need, this can come in handy. Check your business credit reports for accuracy in the same way you check your personal credit score. You can also contact the business credit bureaus to update your company's profile with new information so that the bureau has a more complete history.

21. Identify and Dispute Any Errors.

Use these resources for more than just checking your credit score. Examine the factors that credit bureaus use to assign a rating and look into the ones that have an impact on your score. Errors are all too common. In fact, 25% of these reports contain significant errors. So double-check them. Negative information must be removed as part of your credit repair process. Identify any obvious errors and file a dispute with the credit bureaus, the creditor, or the information source. On the websites of each credit reporting agency, you can file a dispute.

22. Open Additional Credit Lines.

Applying for a new credit card is one way to reduce your credit utilization rates. This results in a hard inquiry, which lowers your credit score in the short term but raises it in the long run due to the additional credit amount. This, in turn, aids your credit repair efforts by increasing your available credit limit, which offsets credit card balances that exceed the 30% prescribed levels. However, if you use the new card to run up a balance, you'll have a problem. Your credit utilization percentage, as well as your credit balances, rises again. However, an increase in your credit limit should lower your utilization rate and improve your credit scores as long as you don't increase your credit card balances. If your business credit is bad or thin, getting a secured business credit card is a good way to rebuild or establish it. When compared to a regular business credit card, a secured business credit card is easier to get approved for, even if you have a bad credit score or a short credit history. Make sure you pay your bills on time because it will appear on your credit report. Take care! Do not apply for multiple credit cards in a short period of time. Your personal credit will be harmed if you make too many "hard" credit pulls.

23. Keep Older Credit Accounts Open.

When you can, pay off existing debts, but don't close the account.

Your oldest accounts are worth a lot of money. The reason for this is that the length of your credit history is a major determinant of your credit score. These accounts should be as old as possible. This is especially true if you haven't made any recent mistakes like late payments or delinquencies. Old accounts can also assist you by lowering your overall credit utilization. If the account is open but has no outstanding balance, the credit utilization percentage will be lower. The importance of credit age is weighted differently by different credit bureaus. For example, FICO considers it to be 15% of the total score. Regardless, maintaining those old accounts will help you improve your credit score.

24. Ensure that your credit mix is diverse.

Your credit score is affected by the amount of credit you have, the balances you owe, and your payment history. It's the same with your credit mix. It can account for up to ten percent of your overall score. What is a credit mix, exactly? It has to do with the amount of credit you have in your profile. Installment and revolving credit are the only two types of credit that apply. Mortgages, car loans, and term loans are examples of installment credit. They have a set end date, and payments are due on a monthly basis. Credit cards and lines of credit are examples of revolving credit. These are accounts with no predetermined end date or monthly payment amount. In an ideal world, you'd like a combination of the two. It shows the ability to handle a variety of accounts. It will be more difficult to improve your score if you only have one or the other.

25. Get Authorized to Use Someone Else's Account.

Adding yourself as an approved user on someone else's credit card account will immediately improve your credit score. Only make sure it's someone with a higher credit score than you! The individual who authorizes your use faces a danger. Registered users are not liable for repaying the debt, according to the statute. The primary consumer bears this responsibility. Furthermore, this type of "piggybacking" credit does not always help the authorizer create credit as well as it does the individual with a low score.

26. Apply for a Secured Bank Loan.

Apply for a secured bank loan if you are unable to receive a loan due to your creditworthiness. A secured loan is one that is backed by something tangible, such as a vehicle, CD, savings account, or piece of equipment. If you can't make your payments, the lender can seize your property, putting you in even more danger. However, making on-time payments for a long period of time will help you improve your credit score.

27. Negotiate to Remove Delinquencies.

Contacting the creditor to try to negotiate a partial payment is one way to erase a derogatory mark on your credit, such as a delinquency. The borrower agrees to reclassify the debt as "paying" in exchange. If you have an agreement, have it in writing and pay only when you have it.

28. Get an Immediate Credit Boost.

According to Experian's website, you can boost your FICO Score "instantly." It's done by Boost, a free opt-in service that lets users connect mobile phone and energy bill data to their credit history. It works by linking their Experian account to the bank account they use to pay their bills. Users should see an immediate improvement in their score if payments are made on time.

You can restore your credit and improve your credit scores, but it will take time and effort. However, you must make credit repair a priority and stick to it. You'll see if you follow the steps mentioned above. The advantages would pay off in the form of capital for your company's expansion. Meanwhile, if you're looking for options when your credit score is poor, take a look at these bad credit business loans.

CHAPTER SIXTEEN: CREDIT CRISIS AND FAILURE

The credit crisis has been related to major declines in real economy output on a scale not seen since World War II, making it a landmark event for global financial markets. The recognition of the recession in 2008 was accompanied by a slew of competing initiatives in response to the credit crisis in 2009 and 2010. A cacophony of dreams, voices, and approaches has resulted. The resulting deluge of information threatens to crowd out the most important concerns regarding the financial crisis. Questions about the relationships between risk, control, and failure are among the most pressing. The credit crisis is an example of a financial market network breakdown. The credit crisis has demonstrated the highly complex and interconnected nature of today's financial markets, as well as the inherent challenges that regulators and industry participants face in managing complex and interconnected risks. The credit crisis also shows that neither industry players nor regulators fully comprehended the underlying financial market risks.

Financial products and markets have become more diverse and global in recent years. While public commentary and policy debates in the wake of the credit crisis centered on the consequences of too-big-to-fail financial services companies, current commentary pays less attention to the network-like features of financial markets and the implications of complex networks for financial markets. The pervasive trading and risk-taking cultures that now characterize many market segments intensify the influence of financial market networks. Individual traders who took on risky trading positions that seriously undermined or, in the case of Baring Brothers, ruined the companies on whose accounts they trade are perhaps the best example of the risk-taking associated with financial market trading activities.

Over-the-counter (OTC) derivatives are a good example of financial innovation as well as the links that bind financial market participants like traders. Derivatives have been a central feature of financial progress, allowing for much more cross-market linkage than at any other point in history. OTC derivatives contracts usually include private legal rules, which are also defined in form documents. OTC derivatives are traded between parties via private contracts based on type agreements that allow for customization of transactional terms. Exchange-traded derivatives, such as futures and options on futures, are purchased and sold in structured derivatives markets and are traded and cleared by standardized contracts. The complexity and investing in financial markets are exemplified by OTC derivatives markets. With a gross market cap of $25 trillion and a notional value of $605 trillion in June 2009, OTC derivatives have become important building blocks in global financial markets. The nature and dynamics of financial markets, not surprisingly, were major factors in the industry and regulatory failures that followed the credit crisis.

Failure, on the other hand, is often debated in the wake of the credit crisis in relation to the financial services firms that many blame for the crisis. While professional financial market participants should bear the brunt of the blame, other failures, including those by regulators, have also played a significant role in the credit crisis. In addition, financial market regulatory mechanisms in the United States have not kept up with financial innovation. Regulators are also unable to provide sufficient risk supervision for the increasingly dynamic trading and other practices that characterize financial markets as a result. The media, elected officials, regulatory agencies, and the general public have all used rhetoric to criticize financial institutions. However, focusing on financial institutions diverts attention away from other shortcomings that led to the credit crisis. Furthermore, few debates devote enough time to addressing the business and regulatory shortcomings that contributed to the credit crisis. The aftermath of the credit crisis may be interpreted as rewarding those who were most responsible for failing to handle or control risky financial market business practices. Industry participants earned government bailouts through programs including the Distressed Asset Relief Program (TARP) and the Public-Private Investment Program (PPIP), which are government efforts to solve issues caused by the inclusion of illiquid and troubled assets on financial institutions' balance sheets. By averting firm collapse, the bailouts have rewarded risk management deficiencies, which has the same important moral hazard consequences that sparked the current financial crisis in the first place. Bailouts reflect the increasingly networked nature of today's financial markets, as well as the potential for firm failures to have a systemic effect. However, since failure is a necessary and desirable business function, preventing failed companies from failing helps to mask the fact that failure can be both necessary and desirable. Furthermore, while deregulation led to the credit crisis, weak regulation and regulatory weakness also played a role. Regulators, like failed market members, may be compensated for their failures by being granted increased regulatory authority. Financial market reform policies will benefit from a greater emphasis on regulatory efficacy as a target and a metric by which to assess regulatory performance, as well as a clearer understanding of the consequences of widespread failures of various market participants and regulators. The institutional and legal ramifications of trading cultures are examined in this essay. It addresses the consequences of trading cultures and considers the regulatory changes that such cultures necessitate. In addition, rather than focusing on mitigating past failures, this Essay proposes adopting regulatory methods that concentrate on preventing potential failures. A strategy for preventing potential failures should involve a number of elements aimed at reducing risk. Creation of mechanisms that force market participants to bear the risks of their actions will be a key component of such a strategy. Various mechanisms, such as insurance, industry bailout pools, and better industry risk management, may be used. These internal industry regulatory efforts should be part of a wider regulatory strategy aimed at building financial market firewalls to minimize the effects of participant failures. To avoid future significant financial market crashes, the US regulatory approach must be fundamentally rethought, as well as regulatory principles that direct regulatory enactment and reform. These regulatory principles should be used to create reliable, effective, flexible, open, and impartial financial market regulatory structures. A central aim of financial market regulation should be to ensure better knowledge of market participants, regulators, and, most importantly, investors. Finally, the global and complex nature of financial markets necessitates regulation based on real market conditions to the maximum degree possible, which necessitates improved data collection and analysis that can be used by investors and regulators to prevent potential financial market meltdowns.

CHAPTER SEVENTEEN: HOW TO GET RID OF CREDIT LOSSES AND ENSURE SAFER BUSINESS

When a company experiences a financial setback as a result of late or non-payments from customers, it can be quite disappointing. It not only has an effect on the company's operations, but it also limits the company's potential growth prospects. Businesses should use credit protection and management systems to have complete control of their credit and collections. Four of the most important benefits of using credit management systems are as follows:1) Covered damages: Credit management and insurance firms provide insurance services to assist in the recovery of losses incurred by credit defaults and delays. This aids companies in lowering their kundf&rluster.

2) Future Growth: The loss coverage gained assists businesses in growing their working capital as well as extending their operations into newer territories.

3) Debt Collection Services: Management companies' debt collection services assist businesses with legal experience and a strong network. 4) Factoring Services: With fakturabelåning, the credit management companies help businesses with increased cash

flow and better payment periods. A third party factoring company purchases the receivables of a company and takes care of the collections and follow-ups. 5) Expert Advice: Credit management firms have detailed information on their customers' credit histories, allowing businesses to make informed decisions based on these reports. Coface is one of the companies that has greatly aided many businesses in operating smoothly. The company operates in many countries and provides detailed and customized solutions based on a company's needs.

17.1 BLAST YOUR BUSINESS CREDIT SCORE!

You should now have a good understanding of how business credit works. Early on in the life of your company, you'll want to concentrate your efforts on establishing business credit. While obtaining business credit takes time, by taking control of your company's credit history, you'll gain a better understanding of how different activities affect your credit rating over time. As a result, there are some tried-and-true approaches you can use if you're wondering how to create business credit quickly. All ten of the measures below will have an effect on your business credit history, hopefully for the better.

1. Register Your Business Entity.

Your company credit history is distinct from your personal credit history, as previously stated. As a result, the first step in establishing business credit is to keep the personal and business finances apart. To keep these finances apart, you'll need to create a registered business company. In terms of beginning a company and handling paperwork, unincorporated business companies such as a general partnership or a sole proprietorship are the easiest to deal with. However, there is no legal or financial distinction between the owner and the company in these arrangements. In this scenario, you'll have to provide your personal social security number while working with a vendor or applying for a loan. As a consequence, your business account operation will appear on your personal credit sheet.

If you want to create business credit, one of the following mechanisms will suffice:

C-corporation – A C-corporation separates you and your company legally and financially. Corporations are treated as legal cities in their own right, and a C-corporation is suitable for a company that plans to issue stock or go public in the future.

S-corporation – An S-corporation is a pass-through entity through which the income of the company are taxed only at the individual level. S-corporations are also called legal entities in their own right.

A limited liability company (LLC) - is a form of incorporated business entity that provides liability protection and financial separation between you and your company. A limited liability company (LLC) is easier to handle than a corporation and provides more tax flexibility.

Limited liability partnership (LLP) - An LLP is a registered business entity that's popular among professional industries, such as lawyers and doctors. While it's crucial to consider your ability to create business credit when deciding how to structure your company, it's not the only thing to think about. You should seek advice from a business attorney or accountant if you're uncertain about which entity form is best for your company.

2. Get an Employer Identification Number (EIN).

Obtaining an EIN is the next step in establishing and building business credit. For tax purposes, the IRS uses an employer identification number (EIN) to track companies. Your EIN serves the same reason for your company as your social security number does for personal taxes. For tax purposes, sole proprietorships, partnerships, and single-owner LLCs may generally use the owner's social security number (as long as they don't have any employees). However, most other forms of businesses need an EIN. Even if you're not expected to get an EIN, it's a good idea to have one anyway.

One of the most important advantages of having an EIN is that it will assist you in establishing business credit. Furthermore, an EIN is free and simple to obtain through the IRS website. When you apply for a loan or a credit card for your company, you'll almost always be asked to provide either your Social Security number or your EIN. If all you have is your social security number, you'll have to rely on your personal credit to apply and get a good rate. As previously mentioned, if you have an EIN, your business credit will be linked to it, and you will be able to use this background to apply for credit products and business financing.

CHAPTER EIGHTEEN: HOW TO CLEAN UP YOUR CREDIT REPORT

Cleaning up your credit reports entails removing incorrect or obsolete records as well as correcting any errors. It does not imply that all delinquent accounts are actually delinquent. Getting rid of something else on the report that has a legal right to be there. Run the other way if an organization claims to be able to "fix your credit" or "clean up your credit report" and thereby miraculously raise your credit score. In reality, you should be able to do it yourself when it comes to removing inaccurate and outdated information from your study.

1. Request your credit reports.

The first step in cleaning up your credit reports is to know where you stand. You should pull your credit reports from all three major credit bureaus Experian, Equifax and TransUnion. Most people will only be concerned with credit reports from the three main CRAs: Equifax, TransUnion, and Experian. You're entitled to one free copy from each agency every 12 months. Also, as of 2020, you can get six free credit reports each year, for seven years, from Equifax. And, in some situations, you can get free copies more often. And you can always pay a small fee for your report, although this usually isn't necessary given all the ways you can get free reports. You should order your report from all three, as they often contain different information. Some people like to stagger the timing, for example, ordering one from Equifax one month, and then ordering one from TransUnion four months later.

There are specialty consumer news agencies in addition to the three national CRAs. Others are used by landlords to monitor details about tenants, while others contain more sensitive information and are used by employers and insurers to track other forms of data. These organizations are also required to provide you with one free annual report. Identifying which ones have a file on you, however, can be difficult. However, if you suspect your prospective landlord would consult a specialist consumer agency, you can inquire about which one he or she consults.

2. Review your credit reports.

After you've obtained your credit reports, go through each one to ensure that the information mentioned is correct. Examine the following factors: Personal details, such as your name and address on your account information, such as balances, credit limits, payment history, and current status (active, inactive, or closed) Bankruptcy and collection data, such as if any of your accounts is marked past due for more than 30 days and sent to a collection agency Examine each of the files thoroughly for something that is incorrect or incomplete.

3. Dispute credit report errors.

You can challenge details about your credit reports electronically with the three national credit reporting agencies, which is the simplest way to do so. If you want, you can write a lengthy letter to the CRA explaining what's wrong and why, as well as attaching supporting documents. You'll have to deliver the letter to the CRA directly. Use the address that the CRA specifies for these conflict letters. These addresses can be found on the agencies' websites. If you find any flaws on your credit report, you can file a lawsuit right away. You can file a lawsuit with the credit bureau that has the incorrect details, which you can do either online or by mail. If the conflict is resolved in your favor, the credit bureau is required by law to notify the other two credit bureaus. However, to be secure, you might want to notify the other two bureaus as well. If your dispute is dismissed, you can either file a written statement that will be included on your credit report, or you can file a complaint with the FTC or the Consumer Financial Protection Bureau. Check out our step-by-step guide to disputing a credit report error for more detail.

4. Make a List and Immediately Address Any Errors or Unsubstantiated Items.

Make a thorough list of anything that is incorrect, incomplete, or obsolete, as well as any missing details. After that, gather evidence. If you closed an account that is still listed as available, for example, see if you can get a letter or other document stating that the account was closed. Before you start cleaning up your negative things, double-check that everything on your credit reports is correct and up to date. This entails double-checking everything from your name and address to your current (and past) accounts. Make sure your information is right and that each account is one you are familiar with. If you discover discrepancies in your credit report, such as a debt that isn't yours, you can file a credit claim with the credit bureaus to have the faulty or unsubstantiated account deleted. The procedure, also known as credit repair, can be completed entirely online via the bureau's website. Many customers have had success hiring a licensed credit repair company to work on their behalf, such as the ones mentioned below. If you have a large number of things to contest, hiring a specialist may be especially beneficial. If you discover any accounts you don't recall opening, addresses you don't know, or other signs of fraud or identity theft, correcting errors as soon as possible is critical. However, mistakes in spelling and numbers should be corrected right away. Your creditors, for example, usually report your account balances to the credit bureaus once a month. An inflated usage rate will lower your credit score if a creditor records a higher balance than you currently have. Credit repair may also be used to fix unverified accounts. There are accounts that a creditor or collection agent does not have the legal authority to recover due to a lack of supporting documentation. You will also have a debt deducted from your records by disputing the account if the collection party cannot prove you owe the debt. Of course, credit restoration would not be able to erase the debt from your accounts if the other party can prove the responsibility for it.

4. Prioritize Overdue and Outstanding Debts.

After correcting any errors or disputable products by credit repair, it's time to get down to business by resolving each remaining negative account one by one. In certain situations, coping with an outstanding debt or high balances and consumption would be essential. If you have outstanding credit card debt, you should work to pay it off as soon as possible, particularly because your credit utilization rate, or the ratio of total debt owed relative to total credit limit, is a significant factor in your credit score. There are several ways you can pay off credit card debt. Here are a few options: Complete a balance transfer: Converting your debt to a card with no interest for up to 21 months would allow you to pay it off faster and for less money than holding it on a high-interest card. The Citi Simplicity Card has one of the best balance transfer intro cycles, at 18 months, followed by a variable APR of 14.74 percent to 24.74

percent. Consolidate debt with a personal loan: Since balance transfer cards often require good or excellent credit, you may want to consider consolidating debt with a personal loan. Personal loans are useful for large sums of debt because they have more lenient credit conditions. Since a personal loan is an installment account (which does not factor into utilization), it will help you lower your credit utilization rate. Credit cards, on the other hand, are revolving accounts that will increase your credit utilization rate (that directly influence utilization).

5. Redeem rewards.

If you've accumulated cash back, points, or miles, you can exchange them for statement credits to cover some of your expenses. Remember that the credit you earn will most likely only cover a portion of your debt, so you may need to combine this option with another, such as a balance transfer card. If you don't have any credit card debt, you can keep paying your bills on time and in full every month. Maintaining a low credit utilization rate, ideally below 10%, is also critical. Consolidating your debt with a personal installment loan is one way to help you get a handle on it.

Consolidation will help you combine various debts into a single loan, preferably one with a lower interest rate than the ones you currently have. Online lending networks, such as the ones mentioned below, make it simple to connect with multiple lenders and find the best deal. Any outstanding debt should be addressed right away. A personal loan will help you pay off (or, in the case of a big debt, pay down) an unpaid debt and bring it current if you can't afford to catch up. You can also contact your creditor directly to see whether an affordable payment schedule can be worked out. Then there's the debt with a high interest rate. Paying down this debt will not only improve your utilization and debt-to-income ratios, but it will also save you money by lowering the amount of interest you pay overall. This frees up money to pay off other loans, helping you to get out of debt even quicker. It's also a good idea to pay off any accounts that are still in collections. While paying off a collection agency-owned debt won't undo the harm done to your reputation by defaulting on it in the first place, a paid collection still looks better to a potential creditor than an unpaid debt. The only exception is if your debt is (extremely) similar to your state's statute of limitations for that form of account. Making a payment to the collection agency will reset the clock on the debt in this situation, so you should think about your options before calling the collection agency.

6. Build a Recent Positive Payment History.

All the low-hanging fruit has been harvested until you've eliminated the inaccuracies, brought your debts current, and consolidated what you can. When it comes to cleaning up your credit, time is your best friend, beginning with building or restoring a recent positive payment history. The most critical element of your credit is your payment history, which can account for up to 35% of your FICO credit score. Given that recent events carry much more weight in scoring models than events from years ago, keeping on track now and in the near future will help you avoid a lot of the trouble. Your choices for new credit would be limited if you have a low credit score, but a low-limit credit card may be a good place to start. Prepare to pay an annual fee and, more than likely, some kind of transaction fee if you prefer an unsecured credit card. A secured credit card could be a better choice if you can come up with the deposit. Creditors want at least six months of good payment history, but a year or more is preferable. This demonstrates that your credit missteps are behind you and that you're making genuine progress toward a brighter financial future. Automating the entire process of using a credit card to build your credit history is a simple way to do so. (It's worth noting that this works best with a card that offers a grace period on new purchase interest charges.)

To begin, set up an automatic payment on your credit card for a small monthly bill, such as a streaming service or your cell phone. Don't use the card for anything else; in fact, consider locking it away in a safe or a locked drawer where it won't be seen. Then, in your bank account, set up automatic payments for that credit card, ideally right after the regular charge appears on your card (but definitely at least several days before your due date each month). Your bank will automatically pay your credit card each month on the date you specify with auto pay. This will guarantee that you do not make a late payment or, worse, miss a payment entirely because it is automatic. Your credit score should increase after around six months of consistent use. When your credit score has improved enough to qualify for a better card, such as one that doesn't charge an annual fee or one that offers incentives, Upgrade your card and repeat the procedure to keep a positive attitude.

7. Regularly Check Your Credit & Track Your Score.

It's one thing to lose weight on a diet and quite another to hold it off, as anyone who has done so will testify. The same can be said for debt and poor credit; you can't clean up your credit and then forget it. Instead, make a habit of checking your credit scores and reports on a regular basis. Make use of your free annual credit reports to ensure that your credit reports are free of mistakes, inaccuracies, and fraudulent accounts. Keep in mind that your credit scores aren't usually included in your free credit reports.

On the plus hand, most credit cards, as well as a range of free third-party providers, provide free monthly or quarterly credit scores. There are also several credit monitoring systems that provide more comprehensive services. Many paying monitoring firms can provide identity safety benefits including Social Security number monitoring in addition to a wide range of credit-building services, such as credit score tracking and credit report warnings. Pricing can vary depending on the services you need, so look around for the best price.

8. Cleaning Up Your Credit Won't Happen Overnight.

Your credit is close to living with white carpet in that if you don't exercise daily care and discipline, you'll end up with a difficult mess to clean up. If you ever have a stain on your carpet, you can't just use any cleaner; you have to scrub it properly or risk damaging it. On the plus side, no matter how much you screw up your credit, you can clean it up (unlike a white carpet, which can quickly become unsalvageable). To restore your credit, all you have to do is recognize the problems, formulate a sound strategy, and fix them one by one. Even the most stubbornly tainted poor credit can be cleaned up with time and effort. Just be patient and understand that it won't happen right away. You could be eligible for a number of benefits after you clean up your credit report. For starters, you won't have any mistakes in your credit report, which will help you improve your credit score. Additionally, if you removed negative information and/or paid off debt, your credit score may improve. Using a balance transfer or a personal loan to pay off credit card debt will also save you money on interest rates. This will free up money for an emergency fund or a high-yield savings account that you might have spent on interest. Having a good credit score and a clean credit report will help you get approved for credit cards, loans, and mortgages, as well as qualify for the best interest rates.

CONCLUSION

While the days of doing business with your bank on a handshake are long gone, you will find that, to a large degree, confidence is still a critical factor when obtaining any type of credit as you gain more experience. As a result, the more you can show a loan officer that you will treat his money/credit responsibly, the more likely you will be granted credit. Providing him with documents such as a written business plan, standard financial statements, and other business tools would go a long way toward demonstrating the ability to responsibly manage business credit. Things in the credit world can start looking pretty grim after a business owner fails in this responsibility, particularly when you need support.

REFERENCE

Berger, A.N., Udell, G.F., 1996. Universal banking and the future of small business lending. In: Saunders, A., Walter, I. (Eds.), Financial System Design: The Case for Universal Banking. Irwin, Burr Ridge, IL, pp. 559±627.

Berger, A.N., Kashyap, A.K., Scalise, J.M., 1995. The transformation of the US banking industry: What a long strange trip it's been. Brookings Papers on Economic Activity 2, 55±218.

Berger, A.N., Saunders, A., Scalise, J.M., Udell, G.F., 1998. The efects of bank mergers and acquisitions on small business lending. Journal of Financial Economics 50, forthcoming.

Bernanke, B.S., Lown, C., 1991. The credit crunch. Brookings Papers on Economic Activity 2, 204±239.

Bizer, D., 1993. Examiners' credit crunch. The Wall Street Journal (March 11) A14. Board of Governors of the Federal Reserve System, 1991±1994. Prime rate charged by banks on short-term business loans. Federal Reserve Bulletin 77±80, July issues.

Brewer III, Genay, H., Jackson III, W., Worthington, P.R., 1996. How are small ®rms ®nanced?

Evidence from small business investment companies. Economic Perspectives, Federal Reserve Bank of Chicago, Chicago, IL, November±December, pp. 2±18.

Calomiris, C.W., Himmilberg, C.P., Wachtel, P., 1995. Commercial paper, corporate ®nance, and the business cycle: A microeconomic perspective. Carnegie±Rochester Conference Series on Public Policy, June, pp. 203±250.

Cole, R.A., Wolken, J.D., 1995. Financial Services Used by Small Businesses: Evidence from the 1993 National Survey of Small

Business Finances. Federal Reserve Bulletin, July, pp. 629±667.

Cole, R.A., Wolken, J.D., Woodburn, L., 1996. Bank and Nonbank Competition for Small Business Credit: Evidence from the 1987 and 1993 National Surveys of Small Business Finances. Federal Reserve Bulletin, November, pp. 983±995. Dun and Bradstreet Corporation, 1994. Various press releases. These data were adapted by the US Small Business Administration, Once of Advocacy. In: The Handbook of Small Business Data, Government Printing Once, Washington, DC, 1994, pp. 263±264.

Dunkelberg, W.C., Dennis Jr., W.J., 1992. The small business `credit crunch'. Working paper, The NFIB Foundation, Washington, DC.

Hall, B.J., 1993. How has the Basle accord affected bank portfolios? Journal of Japanese and International Economies 7 (4), 408±440.

Hancock, D., Wilcox, J.A., 1993. Has there been a ``capital crunch'' in banking? The effects on real estate lending of real estate conditions and bank capital shortfalls. Journal of Housing Economics 3 (1), 31±50.

Hancock, D., Wilcox, J.A., 1994a. Bank capital and the credit crunch: The roles of risk-weighted and un-weighted capital regulations. American Real Estate and Urban Economics Association Journal 22 (1), 59±94.

Afonso, A., P. Gomes and P. Rother. 2007. "What 'Hides' behind Sovereign Debt Ratings?" Working Paper 711. Frankfurt, Germany: European Central Bank.

Campbell, J.Y., A.W. Lo and A.C. Mckinlay, 1997. The Econometrics of Financial Markets. Princeton, United States: Princeton University Press.

Cantor, R., and F. Packer. 1996. "Determinants and Impact of

Sovereign Credit Ratings." Economic Policy Review 2(2): 37-53. New York, United States: Federal Reserve Bank of New York.

Dell'Ariccia, G., I. Schabel and J. Zettelmeyer. 2006. "How Do Official Bailouts Affect the Risk of Investing in Emerging Markets?" Journal of Money, Credit, and Banking 38(7): 1689-1714.

Eichengreen, B., and A. Mody. 1998. "What Explains Changing Spreads on Emerging-Market Debt: Fundamentals Or Market Sentiment?" NBER Working Paper 6408. Cambridge, United States: National Bureau of Economic Research.

González Rozada, M., and E. Levy Yeyati. 2006. "Global Factors and Emerging Market Spreads." Research Department Working Paper 552. Washington, DC, United States: Inter-American Development Bank.

Hausman, J. 1978. "Specification Tests in Econometrics." Econometrica 46(6): 1251-1271.

Lo, A.W., and A.C. McKinlay. 1988. "Stock Market Prices Do Not Follow Random Walks: Evidence from a Simple Specification Test." Review of Financial Studies 1: 41-66.

Powell, A., and J. Martínez. 2007. "On Emerging Economy Sovereign Spreads and Ratings." Research Department Working Paper 629. Washington, DC, United States: Inter-American Development Bank.

Cavalluzzo, KS, Cavalluzzo, LC and Wolken, JD (2002). Competition, Small Business Financing and Discrimination: Evidence from a New Survey, Journal of Business. Vol. 75, Iss. 4, pp. 641-679.

Cole, RA (2008). Who Needs Credit and Who Gets It? Evidence from the 2003 Survey of Small Business Finances. Submitted to the U.S. Small Business Administration, Office of Advocacy, Washington.

Cowan, CD and Cowan, AM (2006). A Survey Based Assessment of Financial Institution Use of Credit Scoring for Small Business Lending. U.S. Small Business Administration. Office of Advocacy. Contract No. SBAH-04-Q-002. Washington.

Francis, B, Hasa, I, and Wang, H (2008). Bank Consolidation and New Business Formation, Journal of Banking & Finance, Vol. 32, Iss. 8, pp. 1598-Freel, MA (2007). Are Small Innovators Credit Rationed? Small Business Economics. Vol. 28, Iss. 1, pp. 23-35. January.

Government Accountability Office (GAO) (2007). Small Business Administration: Additional Measures Needed to Assess 7(a) Loan Program's Performance. GAO-07-769. Washington. July.

Hanc, G (2004). The Future of Banking in America: Summary and Conclusions. FDIC Banking Review. Vol. 16, No. 1, pp. 1- 27.

Hoffmann, M and Shcherbakova, I (2008). Consumption Risk Sharing over the Business Cycle: The Role of Small Firms' Access to Credit Markets. Working Paper No. 363, Institute for Empirical Research in Economics, University of Zurich. March.

Jayaratne, J, and Wolken, J (1999). How Important Are Small Banks to Small Business Lending? New Evidence from a Survey of Small Firms. Journal of Banking and Finance. Vol. 23, Iss. 2-4, pp. 427-458.

Jacobson, T, Lindé, J, and Roszbach, K (2005). Credit Risk versus Capital Requirements under Basel II: Are SME Loans and Retail Credit Really Different?, Journal of Financial Services Research.

Vol. 28, Iss. 1-3, pp. 43-75. October. Previously published as Working Paper No. 162 by the Swedish Riksbank, Stockholm.

Koren, I (2003). The ABCs of Small Business Loan Securitizations: Nothing Small about Small Business in America (2003). Wachovia Securities, Charlotte, NC. March.

Masson, DJ (2007). Commercial Banking in the U.S. versus Canada. Graziadio Business Report. Vol. 10, Iss. 4, http://gbr.pepperdine.edu/074/bank.html Mester, LJ (1997). What's the Point of Credit Scoring? Business Review. Federal Reserve Bank of Philadelphia, pp. 3-16. September/October.

Minniti, M, Bygrave, WD, and Autio, E (2006). Global Entrepreneurship Monitor: 2005 Executive Report. Babson College, Babson Park, MA and London Business School. London.

Bucks, BK, Kennickell, AB, and Moore, KB (2006). Recent Changes in U.S. Family Finances: Evidence from the 2001 and 2004 Survey of Consumer Finances, Federal Reserve Bulletin. Vol. 92, Iss. 1, pp. A1-A38.

Hess, D (2008). SBA Says Loan Demand Is Declining As Economy Slows, Congress Dailey PM, p. 6, October 9.

NFIB Research Foundation (series). Small Business Economic Trends, (eds) Dunkelberg, WC and Wade, H. Washington.

Perelman, M. (1994), Retrospectives: Fixed Capital, Railroad Economics and the Critique of the Market, The Journal of Economic Perspectives, Vol. 8, No. 3, Summer, pp. 189-195.

erelman, M. (1998), The Neglected Economics of Trust, American rnal of Economics and Sociology, Vol. 57, No. 4, October, pp. ˋ89.

n, M. (2006), Railroading Economics: The Creation of the

Free Market Mythology, Monthly Review Press.

Porter, M. (1985), Competitive Advantage, New York: Free Press.

Rosenberg, N. (1982), Inside the Black Box, Technology and Economics, Cambridge University Press.

Scherer, F. (1984), Innovation and Growth, Cambridge, MA: MIT Press.

Schumpeter, J. A. (1912), The Theory of Economic Development, Cambridge: Harvard University Press [1934, 1951, 1961].

Schumpeter, J. A. (1928), The Instability of Capitalism, Economic Journal, Vol. 38, No 151, pp. 361-86.

Schumpeter, J. A. (1939), Business Cycles, New York: McGraw-Hill [1964].

Schumpeter, J. A. (1942), Capitalism, Socialism and Democracy, New York: Harper and Row [1950].

Schumpeter, J. A. (1954), History of Economic Analysis, London: Routledge [1997].

Screpanti, E. and Zamagni, S. (1993), An Outline of the History of Economic Thought, Oxford: Clarendon Press [2003].

Sismondi, L.S. De (1827), Nouveaux principes d'économie politique, Delaunay: Paris.

Stern, K. (1938), Le mouvement cyclique des affaires, Théories allemandes : analyse et critique, Jouve & Co., Paris.

Sweezy, P. (1949), Karl Marx and the Close of His Systmen by Eugen von B&hm-Bawerk & B&hm-Bawerk's criticism of Marx by Rudolf Hilferding, New York: Augustus M. Kelley. te

Velde, R. A. (2001), Schumpeter's Theory of Economic Development Revised, conference 'The Future of Innovation Studies', Eindhoven University of Technology, The Netherlands, 20-23 September. Tugan-Baranowsky, M. v. (1969), Studien zur Theorie und Geschichte der Handelskrisen in England, Scientia Verlag, Aalen.

www.ingramcontent.com/pod-product-compliance
Lightning Source LLC
Chambersburg PA
CBHW070243220526
45465CB00004B/1510